RACING
TOWARD
ARMAGEDDON

WHY ADVANCED TECHNOLOGY
SIGNALS THE END TIMES

Copyright © 2017 Britt Gillette
All rights reserved.
ISBN: 1981968709
ISBN-13: 978-1981968701

Scripture quotations marked (NLT) are taken from the Holy Bible, New Living Translation, copyright © 1996, 2004, 2007 by Tyndale House Foundation. Used by permission of Tyndale House Publishers, Inc., Carol Stream, Illinois 60188. All rights reserved.

RACING TOWARD ARMAGEDDON

WHY ADVANCED TECHNOLOGY
SIGNALS THE END TIMES

BRITT GILLETTE

To Meg.

CONTENTS

Chapter 1 - Introduction 1
Chapter 2 - Armageddon and the End of the World 7
Chapter 3 - God's Overlooked Prophecy 13
Chapter 4 - Peter's Prophecy 19
Chapter 5 - Transhumanism 27
Chapter 6 - Mind Over Matter 33
Chapter 7 - The Coming Global Government 47
Chapter 8 - The Rise of Big Brother 61
Chapter 9 - The Great, Great Depression 67
Chapter 10 - Are You The Messiah? 79
Chapter 11 - The Great Lie 87
Chapter 12 - The War to End All Wars (Man vs. God) 97
Chapter 13 - When Will All These Things Happen? 105
Chapter 14 - Is Technology Our Enemy? 113
About The Author 123

CHAPTER 1

Introduction

WHEN THE DISCIPLES said, "Tell us the signs of your coming and the end of the age" (***Matthew 24:3***), Jesus described a number of signs to look for. He said when those signs appear, His followers will know He's coming. The Old Testament prophets also listed signs. They didn't yet know the name of Jesus. But they referred to the end times and said they would usher in the Messiah's Kingdom.

Today, we see those signs. And according to Jesus, this makes our generation closer to His return than any other. Why do I say this? Because Jesus said, "When you see all these things, you can know my return is near. I'm right at the door" (***Matthew 24:33***). Today, we see the signs Jesus described. We see the signs the prophets said to look for. Many say we don't. They insist the world is the same today as it's always been. But that's just not true.

Generations of Christians lived and died without witnessing *one* of the signs Jesus and the prophets said to look for. That's right. Not a single sign. But our generation? Our generation is witness to *all* of them. So what are these signs? They include:

Israel Back in the Land – God promised to bring the Jewish people back into the land of Israel just before His return (***Jeremiah 23:7-8***). He said He would call them from "among the nations" (***Ezekiel 39:28***), from "the farthest corners of the earth" (***Isaiah 11:12***), and from "north, south, east, and west" (***Psalm 107:3***). He promised to welcome them home from the lands where they were scattered (***Ezekiel 20:34***), and when they returned, He promised to come and establish His everlasting kingdom (***Isaiah 11:11-12***). Rome conquered Israel and scattered the Jewish people across their vast empire. But in 1948, God kept His promise and restored the nation of Israel.

The Jews Back in Jerusalem – Jesus said armies would surround Jerusalem, destroy the city, and enslave its citizens. This happened in A.D. 70 when the Roman legions did exactly that. Jesus then said people other than the Jews would control Jerusalem for a time, then the Jewish people would once again control Jerusalem. When this happened, Jesus promised to return (**Luke 21:24-28**). For 1,897 years, non-Jews ruled the city. Then, in 1967, the Jewish people once again took control of Jerusalem.

The Gospel Preached Throughout the World – When asked about the end of the age and the signs of His coming, Jesus said to look for a very specific sign. He said the Gospel will be preached throughout the entire world. Every nation will hear it. And then? And then, the end will come (***Matthew 24:14***). For centuries after the crucifixion, the Gospel was confined to a small geographic area surrounding the Mediterranean Sea. In the past two centuries, an evangelistic explosion has brought the Gospel to every nation in the world. Today, missionaries are in every nation. The Bible is translated in hundreds of languages, and radio, TV, satellite, and Internet ministries send the message of Jesus around the world. Our generation is literally on the verge of spreading the Gospel to every last person on earth.

An Increase in Travel and Knowledge – Six hundred years before Jesus, an angel gave a special message to the prophet Daniel. He said "travel and knowledge" will increase in the end times (***Daniel 12:4***). For centuries of human history, dramatic gains in travel and knowledge did NOT take place. Yet the last two hundred years have seen explosions in the speed and frequency of travel as well as the amount and availability of knowledge.

Arrival of the Exponential Curve – Jesus said a variety of global signs will mark His return and the end of the age. These include spiritual, natural, societal, and political signs. He said they will appear in a distinct way – like birth pains (***Matthew 24:3-8***). This means the frequency and intensity of these signs will increase as His return nears. Our generation has seen the exponential increase in war, famine, and earthquakes Jesus said to look for. In the

20th Century alone, more people died from war and famine than lived on the entire earth when Jesus spoke these words.

Israel Surrounded by Enemies – The Bible says enemies will surround Israel in the end times. Those enemies will say "Come, let us wipe away the nation of Israel. Let's destroy the memory of its existence" (***Psalm 83:4***) and "Let us take for ourselves these pasturelands of God" (***Psalm 83:12***). Ezekiel said Israel's neighbors will say "God has given their land to us" (***Ezekiel 11:14-17***), and "Israel and Judah are ours. We will take possession of them. What do we care if their God is there?" (***Ezekiel 35:10***). Since the rebirth of Israel in 1948, the daily headlines have included these Bible verses. Israel's Muslim neighbors claim the land of Israel for themselves, and they have no regard for the God of Israel.

Israel's Exceedingly Great Army – Ezekiel said, in the end times, Israel will field *"an exceedingly great army"* (***Ezekiel 37:10***). Zechariah said Israel will be like a fire among sheaves of grain, burning up the neighboring nations (***Zechariah 12:6***) and even the weakest Israeli soldier will be like David (***Zechariah 12:8***). Since 1948, Israel has fought no less than four conventional wars against its neighbors. Despite being outnumbered more than 50 to 1, Israel has experienced overwhelming victory every time.

The Rise of the Gog of Magog Alliance – The Bible says a military alliance that includes Russia, Iran, Turkey, and a number of Muslim nations will attack Israel "in the latter days" (***Ezekiel 38:8***) when God brings His people home from among the enemy nations (***Ezekiel 39:27***). Today, we see those very nations coming together – an alliance that has never existed in world history.

The Rise of a United Europe – The Bible says a revived Roman Empire will come to power in the end times (***Daniel 2***, ***Daniel 7***, ***Revelation 17***). According to Daniel, it will be a ten nation alliance of weak and strong nations. Some parts will be as strong as iron, while other parts will be as weak as clay (***Daniel 2:42***). We see the beginning of this alliance in the European Union – a coalition of weak and strong nations struggling to stay together.

The Rise of Global Government – The Bible says in the last days a single government will rule the world politically (***Revelation 13:7***), religiously

(***Revelation 13:8***), and economically (***Revelation 13:16-17***). It will rule over "all people, tribes, and languages" on the face of the earth (***Revelation 13:7***). Its authority will be so complete no one will be able to buy or sell anything without its permission (***Revelation 13:16-17***). For centuries, a true global government was impossible. Today, world leaders openly discuss it.

Denial of the Signs – Almost two thousand years ago, Peter issued a warning. He said in the last days people will mock the idea of Jesus returning. They'll make fun of those who believe in the Second Coming and say exactly what we hear today – things like, *"I thought Jesus was coming back? What happened to His promise? Generation after generation has said He's coming. Yet, since the beginning of the world, everything has remained the same!"* (***2 Peter 3:3-4***).

This Generation

Despite the naysayers, Jesus *is* coming, and our generation will witness His return. The convergence of these signs proves it. Jesus Himself said, "***When all these things begin to happen***, look up for your salvation is near!" (***Luke 21:28***). In fact, He said the generation witnessing these signs will not pass away before He returns (***Matthew 24:34***). The signs Jesus said to look for are present in our generation. And this is unprecedented in human history.

Now, you may not think that's a big deal. After all, for years I've heard people say something similar to what Peter said they would say – *"Every generation has thought Jesus is coming back, but He hasn't."* This implies Jesus isn't coming back because he hasn't come back yet. But just because something ***hasn't*** happened, does that mean it will ***never*** happen? Of course not. Moreover, this line of thinking completely ignores the arrival of so many signs. Signs prophesied thousands of years ago.

Think about it. For over 1,800 years of Christianity, ***not one*** of these signs was present. Take a moment to let that sink in. Eighteen centuries passed. Just shy of two thousand years – and not a single sign of His return. But today? Today, the signs are everywhere you turn.

This is why we can be confident Jesus is coming soon. We can see all the signs of His return appearing together. This convergence of signs is the #1 prophetic sign – the #1 reason to believe Jesus is right at the door. Both Jesus and the prophets told us about those signs, and the appearance of just one is reason enough to take notice. But the arrival of one sign after another? That should really get your attention.

YET ANOTHER SIGN

Given all these signs, it's no coincidence a recent trend also points to the soon return of Jesus. In fact, it does more than just point. It screams out, "Jesus is coming!" So what is this trend? If you haven't guessed already, it's the breakneck speed of advanced technology.

Every year, the power of our technology increases by leaps and bounds. Every year, the cost goes down. And the exponential advance of technology signals the end of this age. Why do I say that? This is why… While God's Word is never dependent on human actions for fulfillment, if certain technological trends continue, they will without a doubt lead to the fulfillment of many end times bible prophecies.

Given the signs we see today and the nearness of His return, advanced technology is likely to play a major role in the rise of the Antichrist, global government, and the final battle to close out this age. After all, if advanced technology were the only sign, we would have little cause for concern. But it's not. Israel is back in the land… The Jews are back in Jerusalem… Though small, Israel has an exceedingly great army… Europe is unifying… And the Gospel is being preached to the ends of the earth. These are the very signs Jesus and the prophets said to look for. And again, our generation is the first *ever* to witness these signs.

But aside from all that, ours is the first generation to witness something else. Ours is the first generation able to foresee the fulfillment of certain end times bible prophecies outside of a supernatural fulfillment. For example, we can see how advanced technology could bring these prophecies closer to reality:

- Total control of the world economy (***Revelation 13:7***)
- World government (***Revelation 13:7***)
- The whole world watching an event at the same time (***Revelation 11:9***)
- Instant destruction of one-third of mankind (***Revelation 9:18***)
- And more…

Chapter 1

For centuries, Christians found these prophecies hard to understand. But today? Today, we can easily see how they're possible outside of the supernatural. In fact, as with the previous signs, no other generation of Christians can say this.

Where We're Headed

All these signs point in one direction. Advanced technology does too. While the crucifixion and resurrection of Jesus are the climax and focal point of human history, His return is the climax of the end of this age. All the end times events outlined in the Bible point to it. They warn of a day of judgment (*Joel 3:2*), and the Bible describes this time using many names. However, the world knows it by one name and one name only. A single word on the tongues of believers and non-believers alike – Armageddon.

CHAPTER 2

Armageddon and the End of the World

IN THE 1998 movie *Armageddon*, a massive asteroid is on course to strike the earth and kill everyone in the world. In order to save the planet, the heroes of the movie jump on a rocket, blast into space, and destroy the asteroid with a nuclear bomb. The world averts disaster, and everyone cheers.

This is typical of what most people imagine when they think of Armageddon. And the movie *Armageddon* is typical of what Hollywood thinks too. We see it over and over. Just replace the asteroid with a comet, and you've got a new Armageddon movie. Or you can replace the asteroid/comet with a super virus run amuck, a global nuclear war, or global warming. I could go on and on, but you get the point.

All these movies show one thing – people are fascinated with the end of the world. And it's not just Christians who take an interest in Armageddon.

CONCERN OVER ARMAGEDDON

Today's interest in end-of-the-world scenarios should come as no surprise. While such speculation dates back to the dawn of time, the 20th Century accelerated our worst fears. World War I brought carnage and destruction on a scale few imagined. Yet World War II soon surpassed it. Throw in the development of nuclear weapons and decades of Cold War tension, and it's easy to see why end-of-the-world speculation has intensified.

For the first time ever, mankind has the destructive capacity to kill billions

Chapter 2

of people through use of chemical, biological, or nuclear weapons. People are also more aware of the potential threat posed by viruses, stray comets, and asteroids. And the human imagination continues to run wild with thoughts of invading aliens, cataclysmic global warming, and wild conspiracy theories of world domination.

These end-of-the-world scenarios have prompted a number of people to speculate Armageddon is at hand. The climax of the end times period prophesied in the Bible – the Battle of Armageddon – has taken on a life of its own outside of its biblical context. Politicians, scientists, and world leaders routinely warn against it. Hollywood blockbusters and apocalyptic thrillers constantly invoke it. Everywhere you turn, you can find reference to Armageddon. In fact, references to Armageddon are so widespread, almost everyone in the world has heard of it. Even those who have never read the Bible.

Think about that. What pops into *your* head when you think of Armageddon? What mental images does it conjure? When most people think of Armageddon, they imagine the destruction of the entire human race and the end of the world. Because of this, the word Armageddon is forever linked with all-out nuclear war, devastating natural disasters, killer comets or asteroids striking the earth, or any number of dire, large-scale threats to human civilization.

Before I read the Bible, I used to think the same thing. After all, we're bombarded with media messages reinforcing these beliefs. The idea Armageddon is the end of the world has been conventional wisdom for many years. But you know what? I don't care what conventional wisdom says. I care what the Bible says. Does the Bible link Armageddon to nuclear bombs, comets, asteroids or global warming? Is that really what the Bible says?

When I first studied the Bible, I believed it did. But I soon learned otherwise. In fact, the Bible doesn't connect a single one of these destructive events with Armageddon.

What the Bible Says

The Armageddon of the Bible has nothing to do with Bruce Willis and killer earthbound asteroids. It isn't about global warming, and it doesn't involve nuclear war. So if that's the case, what is Armageddon?

Believe it or not, Armageddon is a place – a real geographic location.

The word Armageddon only appears once in the New Testament (***Revelation 16:16***). It's a Greek translation of the Hebrew name for a place in Israel called Megiddo. For centuries, Megiddo served as the location of numerous ancient battles – a strategic location along an ancient trade route linking several empires.

Megiddo is historically important, but it plays an even more important future role. What's so special about it? Megiddo (or Armageddon as the world knows it) will be the gathering place for the largest and most destructive battle in human history.

According to the Bible, all the armies of the world will one day gather at Armageddon in preparation for this battle. And what the Bible says they do once they arrive will surprise most people.

The End of the World?

Pop culture tells us when the armies of the world gather together at Armageddon, the end of the world is at hand. Everywhere we turn, people seem to be in agreement. *"Look at all the things that are happening,"* they say. *"The end of the world is coming!"* But is that really the case? I don't think so, and I would advise anyone to avoid such dire predictions. In fact, I won't make any predictions at all. Instead, I'll issue a bold proclamation. Are you ready for it? Here it is:

"The world will NOT come to an end – *ever.*"

How can I be so sure? After all, I'm no prophet. Nevertheless, I'm absolutely positive the world will never come to an end. The reason I'm so sure? The Bible says so. And I'm confident its future prophecies will be fulfilled just as precisely as those in the past.

Keep in mind when I say the world will never end, I mean the earth itself will never be destroyed. I also mean the human race will live on forever. Now I realize most people don't share these beliefs, but that doesn't matter. The Bible is clear on both points. It says both the earth and people will continue on long after the Battle of Armageddon.

Chapter 2

The End of the Age

Now, while the Bible says the arrival of Armageddon does not bring the end of the world, it does say this present *age* will come to an end. What does that mean? It means the world as we know it will not go on forever. All the things we hate about this world – war, greed, lust, murder, jealousy, injustice, and all the evils of this world – they will come to an abrupt end. A new age will begin. One of love, peace, justice, mercy, and kindness.

This new age will come about in the aftermath of the world's most infamous battle – Armageddon. Does that surprise you? If so, it's because today's media has conditioned us to believe otherwise.

But here's what the Bible says. The Bible says one day all the armies of the world will gather together at Armageddon to do battle (**Revelation 16:16**). And when they do, they **will not** destroy each other and the world **will not** come to an end (**Psalm 78:69**).

Did you catch that? Contrary to popular belief, the battle of Armageddon does not result in human extinction. And contrary to what many Christians believe, God doesn't intervene at Armageddon in order to stop humanity from destroying itself. He intervenes for another reason. How do I know? Again, it's not because I'm a prophet. It's because I've read the Bible.

Why Armageddon Matters

If I'm telling the truth about the Battle of Armageddon and what the Bible says about it… And if it's true Armageddon only ushers in the end of an age and not the end of the world, then why is Armageddon so important? If human beings don't destroy each other, or even come close to the brink of destroying each other, isn't that a bit anticlimactic? You might think so. But once again, conventional wisdom is far from reality. In fact, what the Bible says about Armageddon is an even bigger deal than almost anyone thinks.

The truth about Armageddon has been in the Bible from day one, sitting in plain view of generation after generation of Christians. Yet most believers gloss over it. They never give it a second thought. Why? Because the true story of Armageddon is hard to accept. It's so outlandish, most people dismiss it on sight. You'll soon realize why.

Trust me, when you read what the Bible says, your first instinct will probably be denial. I understand. But I encourage you to keep an open mind. If you do, I believe you'll see the events of our time in a whole new light.

So now you're probably wondering, *"What? What is it? What is this 'plain view' truth about Armageddon?"* To understand, we need to revisit one of the most well-known stories in the Bible. In fact, it's such a well-known story it's often overlooked for what it really is. What is it?

It's a prophecy – a prophecy of things to come.

CHAPTER 3

God's Overlooked Prophecy

AS A CHILD, I never attended Sunday school. Nevertheless, I couldn't help but learn many of the stories found in the Bible. What child doesn't know the story of Noah's Ark? David and Goliath? Or Adam and Eve? Almost everyone is familiar with these popular Bible stories.

One such story is the Tower of Babel. If you grew up in church, you're familiar with this story. But even if you've never spent a single minute in church, I bet you've seen depictions of the tower and know the basic elements of the story. Regardless of how deep your knowledge of the Bible is, it's a safe bet you've heard it. And most likely, you can tell me the whole story right now with no need to consult a Bible.

But let me ask you this. How well do you *really* know it?

I would argue most people, including most Christians, don't really know the Tower of Babel story at all. Because most people fail to ask themselves the two most important questions:

#1) What's this story about?

and

#2) What's this story trying to tell us?

So let's revisit the story, and then try to answer these questions.

Chapter 3

THE TOWER OF BABEL

According to the Bible, here's what happened several thousand years ago:

> *"At one time the whole world spoke a single language and used the same words. As the people migrated eastward, they found a plain in the land of Babylonia and settled there. They began to talk about construction projects. 'Come,' they said, 'let's make great piles of burnt brick and collect natural asphalt to use as mortar. Let's build a great city with a tower that reaches to the skies - a monument to our greatness! This will bring us together and keep us from scattering all over the world.' But the Lord came down to see the city and the tower the people were building. 'Look!' he said. 'If they can accomplish this when they have just begun to take advantage of their common language and political unity, just think of what they will do later. Nothing will be impossible for them! Come, let's go down and give them different languages. Then they won't be able to understand each other.' In that way, the Lord scattered them all over the earth; and that ended the building of the city. That is why the city was called Babel, because it was there that the Lord confused the people by giving them many languages, thus scattering them across the earth."*
> **Genesis 11:1-9** (NLT)

WHY THIS MATTERS

At this point you might be thinking, *"Okay, Britt. So what? I've heard this story dozens of times. What's the big deal?"* I understand why you might think that. But did you notice anything different? Remember, most people who read the Tower of Babel story fail to ask themselves what it's about and what it's trying to tell us. So I hope you paid extra attention when you read it this time.

If so, have you thought about how you would answer those two questions? I think when you do, you'll see exactly why the Tower of Babel is a prophecy of things to come.

Let's start with what the people were doing. Do you remember why they started building the Tower of Babel in the first place? That's right. They were building a monument to their ***own*** greatness.

Okay. So what, right? People do this all the time. We build skyscrapers and monuments all over the planet, each one trying to outdo the others in terms of height and opulence. What makes the Tower of Babel any different?

While it may not be significant to us, it was to God. As soon as He saw the tower being built, He immediately scattered the people and confused their languages. Why? Why didn't He just destroy the tower and send the builders home? The Bible tells us the answer, and it's the key to understanding why this story is a prophecy of things to come.

God's reaction reveals a lot, because something concerned the God of the Universe so much He took immediate action to end it right then and there. What was it? What was so important, God had to put an immediate stop to it?

What concerned Him was this:

"Nothing would be impossible for them" (**Genesis 11:6**).

Did you catch that? If not, I'll repeat it.

"*Nothing* would be impossible for them."

Nothing? That's right – nothing. So what does this mean? Simply put, it means when the human race is united with a common language and a common purpose, "nothing" will be impossible for them.

God's Warning

In the Tower of Babel story, God scatters the human race and confuses them with different languages. In doing so, He specifically eliminates two aspects of human civilization at that time:

1) global government, and
2) a common language

Why do these things concern Him? God flat out tells us. He says, in due time, if they're allowed to continue, "nothing will be impossible" for humans. This is more than an offhand remark. It's a prophecy of things to come.

It's a prophecy of something so bad, God put a stop to it the moment He

Chapter 3

first saw it. God knew that – left to pursue its technological development – the human race would one day challenge Him. After all, what was the motive for building the Tower of Babel in the first place?

> *"Let's build a great city with a tower that reaches to the skies - a monument to our greatness!"* **Genesis 11:4** (NLT)

The human race set out to build a monument to its own greatness, exalting itself above God and extending its tower far into heaven. But to what purpose? With the sole purpose of seizing God's glory and authority. Now, let me ask you another question.

Do you think this desire ended with the Tower of Babel?

No. It didn't. In fact, it continues to this day. And soon it will result in one final attempt to overthrow God's authority. Given technology's exponential advance, that day will come sooner than most people think.

The Bible reveals a united mankind will try to fulfill a desire it's had since the Garden of Eden – a desire to place itself equal to or higher than God. As humans, we think quite highly of ourselves. Can you recall a time when you've overestimated your abilities? Or a time when you acted out of complete self-centeredness? I can. We all can. It's in our nature.

Remember, the whole purpose of the Tower of Babel was to build a monument to the greatness of the human race – not to honor God. This desire to raise ourselves higher than the heavens is a universal and time-honored tradition. We're arrogant. We believe we can blaze our own trail and make our own way. Many of us believe we don't need God. And eventually, this desire to raise ourselves higher than the heavens will lead to a massive worldwide conflict – a battle known as Armageddon.

WHAT ARMAGEDDON REALLY IS

For some reason, entire generations have misunderstood Armageddon. It's not a battle between the armies of this world. Yes, Armageddon is the gathering place for a literal physical battle. But that battle is not between the rival armies of this world. It's between the people of this world and God Almighty.

That's right. Armageddon is a battle between human beings and the God of the Universe. Find that hard to believe? Most people do. That's why other interpretations have been popularized. But, in plain language, that's what the Bible says. Mankind will literally take up arms in a physical war against the God of Abraham, Isaac, and Jacob.

Still don't believe me? I don't blame you. I wouldn't take my word for it either. So go to your Bible, where you'll find some passages like these (emphasis mine):

"These miracle-working demons caused all the rulers of the world ***to gather for battle against the Lord*** on that great judgment day of God Almighty." ***Revelation 16:14*** (NLT)

"Then I saw the beast gathering the kings of the world and their armies in order ***to fight against the one sitting on the horse and his army.*** " ***Revelation 19:19*** (NLT)

The gathering of the world's armies at Armageddon is preparation for an act of war. But the armies aren't preparing to wage war against each other. Read again what Revelation 19:19 says. They gather together in order to plot against "the one sitting on the horse and his army." Who is the "one sitting on the horse"?

Jesus Christ.

Are you beginning to see why the Battle of Armageddon is such a big deal? Despite the popular myths, Armageddon is not the final realization of Cold War fears of nuclear annihilation. It's not the conventional armies of the world gathering to fight each other to the death.

The end goal of Armageddon is for the human race to break free from God's authority. Impossible, right? I think this is why so many people have "spiritualized" these passages. The whole idea seems preposterous. People tell themselves, *"Of course it doesn't mean a literal battle. It's symbolic. The forces of good vs. evil."* Yet that's our own minds talking. It's not what the Bible says. Over and over again, the Bible describes this battle in clear terms.

For example, Psalm 2 has this to say:

"Why are the nations so angry? Why do they waste their time with futile plans? The kings of the earth prepare for battle; the rulers plot together

Chapter 3

> ***against the Lord and against His Anointed One***. *'Let us break their chains,' they cry. 'And free ourselves from slavery to God.' But the one who rules in heaven laughs. The Lord scoffs at them."* **Psalm 2:1-4** *(NLT)*

Notice once again who the rulers plot against. They don't plot against each other or Israel. They plot against "the Lord and His Anointed One." Who is the "Lord's Anointed One"? Again, it's Jesus Christ. The armies of the world plot against the Prince of Peace Himself!

Does this sound far-fetched? It should. After all, mankind would have to become infinitely more powerful than it is now before it could ever challenge God. But you know what? That power is coming. And you know what else?

Jesus Himself described it.

CHAPTER 4

Peter's Prophecy

TWO THOUSAND YEARS ago, Peter said in the last days people will mock and ridicule those who look forward to the Second Coming. They'll say something along the lines of, *"Oh Jesus promised to come back, did He? Christians have said that for almost 2,000 years now. Yet things are the same today as they've been for thousands of years"* (**2 Peter 3:3-4**).

Again, for years now, I've heard people say something similar. And I'll wager you've heard people say something similar too. Maybe you've said it yourself. But you know what?

It's completely untrue.

And of course we hear this same argument used in regard to Armageddon as well. It makes sense because Armageddon and the Second Coming of Jesus are linked together. The argument usually goes something like this, *"The end of the world? People have been saying that for centuries, but it hasn't happened yet. The world goes on the same as always."*

Unfortunately, I hear this repeated over and over again. But think about how absurd it is. How is today the same as it's been for thousands of years? The exact opposite is true. Today is unlike any other time in human history, and no other generation has been more likely to witness Armageddon and the Second Coming.

Chapter 4

The Pace of Change

I can point to countless areas where our life today is dramatically different than life for past generations. But the one area with the most dramatic difference is technology.

Think about it. For thousands of years, man could travel no faster than a horse could carry him. This remained true from the Garden of Eden until the 19th Century. That's a long time! Yet, in the short span of a century and a half, we've upgraded to automobiles that go from zero to 60 mph in a matter of seconds. We've gone from men publicly proclaiming manned flight is impossible to jet airplanes traveling several times the speed of sound.

Does all this make you think the world is "the same now as it's always been"? I doubt it.

Think about the technology that's probably within ten feet of you right now. For example, you're most likely reading this book on a phone, tablet, or ereader. Each of those devices has the capability to store thousands of books – the equivalent of a small library one hundred years ago. And such devices are affordable to almost everyone. Compare that to a two thousand book home library a century ago. Only the rich could afford such luxury.

And this revolution isn't confined to books. It's the same with music. Mozart lived less than 250 years ago. Kings, queens, and the wealthy elite commissioned him to create original scores and entertain them with his musical abilities. Then they paid entire orchestras to gather together and perform for them. Today? You carry around more music on your iPod than they likely ever heard in a lifetime. And you can play it on demand whenever you want.

Look at how warfare has changed. For centuries, battles consisted of hand-to-hand combat. Warriors used shields, swords, spears, and daggers. Sometimes they used horses, catapults, and gunpowder. As warfare evolved over the course of centuries, very little changed in terms of how much damage a single weapon could inflict.

The 20th Century changed all of that. World War I introduced new rapid fire weapons, TNT, and chemical weapons. These led to the mass slaughter of armies. And World War II? World War II brought gas chambers and systematic genocide on a mass scale. It also gave us the atomic bomb – a single weapon capable of destroying an entire city.

And today? Today, we have drones flying high above the battlefield. They kill enemy combatants who often don't even know they're being targeted.

Still think "things are the same as they've always been?" I don't. After thousands of years in which human travel options basically stayed the same, we went from the Wright Brothers to men on the moon in less than seven decades. After thousands of years of slow and incremental innovations in warfare, human beings are now capable of killing every person on the planet.

It's clear to any reasonable person the past two centuries, and the past few decades in particular, stand in stark contrast to all previous human history. It's not a debate. It's a fact.

The extraordinary pace of technological change is the story of our time, yet most people take it for granted. They've grown used to it. But if you study history, you'll realize how massive the change is. Our time is like no other, and our time is one of the most important in all of human history. Not because of new technology or astounding developments, but because of the *way* technology is advancing. The exponential growth of our technology is a sign. It's a sign Armageddon and the end of the age are upon us.

Where do I get this idea? Where else? The Bible. And no one less than Jesus Himself told us to be on the lookout for this exact moment in time.

Jesus and the Exponential Curve

Nearly 2,000 years ago, the disciples came to Jesus with a simple question, "What will be the signs of your coming and the end of the age?" They longed for Jesus to establish His everlasting Kingdom. What signs should they look for? How will they know it's near? In response, Jesus described the signs of His Coming and immediately compared them to birth pains (***Matthew 24:8***).

So what did Jesus mean when He said the signs of His Coming will resemble the pains of a woman in labor? He meant that, just like birth pains, the signs He mentioned will appear with greater frequency and intensity as we approach the end. These signs include the appearance of false messiahs, wars, rumors of war, famines, and earthquakes (***Matthew 24:4-7***).

You'll notice not one of these signs is unique to any one generation. So how can they possibly indicate the end of the age? The answer is simple. They only indicate the time of the end when they appear like labor pains. In other words, just as labor pains increase in frequency and intensity as a birth gets closer, the signs Jesus mentioned will also increase in frequency and intensity as His Coming draws near.

If you were to plot events on a graph that increase in both frequency and intensity over time, do you know what that graph will look like? That's right. An exponential curve.

Now remember, Jesus didn't limit the signs to false messiahs, wars, famines, pestilence, persecution, and earthquakes. He said those signs will only mark "the beginning of birth pains." Jesus was really pointing to a pattern. He was telling us to look for the exponential curve, and when we see the curve, we can know one thing - He's coming. And you know what? Today, we see the curve.

If you chart human population growth over the last 2,000 years, can you guess what it looks like? That's right. An exponential curve. But why? The primary reason is technological advancement. Only through exponential advances in technology, particularly in the areas of farming and medicine, can the planet support such a large number of people. And of course, the exponential increase in world population brings with it increases in the frequency and intensity of wars and famines.

The prophet Daniel also described the exponential curve. An angel told him to seal up the words of his book until "the end times" when "travel and knowledge will increase" (**Daniel 12:4**). If we're in the times Jesus described – times comparable to labor pains – then we should expect to see exponential increases in both travel and knowledge. Is this what we see? You bet.

As mentioned earlier, we went from the Wright Brothers taking a twelve second flight in a glider to men on the moon in less than two generations. If that's not an exponential increase in travel, I don't know what is!

And what about knowledge? Do we see exponential increases in knowledge? Yes. When it comes to the accumulation of knowledge and information, we see great strides made on a daily basis.

Need an example? In 1990, there was only one website. Think about that. Think of how much the world has changed in such a short period of time. Only one website in 1990. Six years later, the Internet had more than one hundred thousand. A decade later? *One hundred million.* As of this writing, estimates exceed one billion. And that number will be out of date by the time you read this.

Technological Advancement

This rapid advance in technology shows no sign of ending. Every day, more people gain access to the Internet, new information is distributed, and new breakthroughs take place in almost every area of life. Computers continue to increase in power and decline in cost. And advances in artificial intelligence become more impressive. For example, in 2011, an IBM computer named Watson defeated former *Jeopardy!* champions Brad Rutter and Ken Jennings. Yet, **within months**, Watson was obsolete.

Where is all this going? The trend points to more and more automation and less need for human labor – both physical and mental. By itself, this is a good thing. It raises everyone's standard of living, increases leisure time, and creates more time to explore our creativity.

But with each passing day, the exponential curve becomes more vertical in nature. The closer it gets to going vertical, the closer we get to the end of the age. So it shouldn't surprise you to learn many people who predict technological trends for a living **also** claim we're on an exponential curve. And many believe the curve will go vertical in our lifetime. In fact, there's a name for it.

The Singularity

In tech circles, this point in time is known as "the singularity." So what is the singularity?

In simple terms, it's a future point in time when the change around us is so rapid, we can no longer follow it. In other words, technology will become so powerful (and the change around us become so rapid) the world will simply pass us by. In a sense, *we* will become obsolete. Sound hard to believe? It shouldn't.

Think of how quickly things change now. How many times have you learned how to use your new phone, computer, or TV only to learn a new model is out? That the one you finally mastered is now obsolete? How many times have you learned a new software package, only to see a new version released a month later? This happens a lot doesn't it?

Well, these examples give us a glimpse at the type of change the singularity promises to bring.

Advances in technology aren't taking place in a straight line. They're taking place exponentially. For example, conventional wisdom tells us the next 100 years will bring the same amount of progress as the last 100 years. If that's right, the next 100 years will bring great change. But is that what the next 100 years will bring?

Those who believe in the singularity say no. And all indications say they're right. If technology continues to advance exponentially, the next 100 years will bring more like twenty times the progress we saw in the 20th Century! Can we even begin to understand what that means? Imagine the impact. What will such change mean for people, industries, and entire nations? You might think we'll easily adapt. After all, if technology continues to advance at the same exponential rate, what's the problem? Hasn't change been a part of life for centuries?

It has, and we've become used to change. In fact, many embrace it and look forward to it. But change will be different as we approach the singularity. Because the pace at which change occurs will be much faster.

For example, the Industrial Revolution took place over 200 to 250 years. During that time, jobs and industries became obsolete, the balance of world power shifted, and the death toll of war significantly increased. The Industrial Revolution raised the standard of living and proved to be a net gain for humanity, but it wasn't painless.

What will the world look like if similar change takes place in a single decade? Would *you* be able to adapt?

WHEN WILL THE SINGULARITY TAKE PLACE?

We don't know for sure when the singularity will take place. Many futurists have noted their belief in the nearness of it, with quite a few predicting it for our generation. Some think it will arrive in this century, while others think it's still hundreds of years away.

If we continue at the same exponential pace – developing advanced technologies like quantum computers, artificial intelligence, and genetic engineering – it's near certain we'll witness the singularity in this century.

At this point, you might be thinking to yourself, *"That's interesting. But what does any of this have to do with Armageddon, the Second Coming, and the Tower of Babel?"*

Everything.

In fact, the singularity answers the most perplexing question of Armageddon:

How do humans become so powerful they're able to do battle with God Himself?

A Return to Babel

The singularity (and the rapid pace of technological change that comes with it) will accelerate a number of recent developments. For example, international travel is more commonplace today than it was one hundred years ago. And in the years to come, it will be even more commonplace. As the cost of new technologies decrease, developing nations will quickly adopt them. When they do, more and more people will plug into the global economy. More and more people will log onto the Internet. Eventually, everyone in the world will be connected.

Advances in artificial intelligence will lead to near perfect language translation software. This will break down language barriers and lead to greater cooperation among people of different nations. And of course, greater cooperation will further accelerate the arrival of new technological breakthroughs.

For example, imagine a device similar to a hearing aid that acts as a foreign language translator. I talk to you in English. You hear me in Japanese. You talk back to me in Japanese. I hear you in English. Sound like science fiction? Not long ago, smartphones sounded like science fiction. Such a device will come in our lifetime, and when it does, the language barriers dividing the world since the Tower of Babel will disappear.

When that happens, the obstacles to world government and a united humanity will also disappear for the first time since the Tower of Babel. And what did God Himself tell us in the Tower of Babel story? That if human beings retain the same language and a united purpose, "**nothing will be impossible**" for them. And "nothing" includes a direct physical confrontation with the God of the Universe.

CHAPTER 5

Transhumanism

IN THE HOLLYWOOD film franchise *Terminator*, humans create computers so powerful they decide to take over. War breaks out between the humans and the "machines" – with an advanced artificial intelligence in control of the machines. Is this where we're headed? Is such a scenario possible? Some say yes. They say, "Humans will soon be obsolete."

I argue they're wrong. After all, who's greater – the creator or the created (**Isaiah 45:9-10**)? While it's certainly **possible** for advanced computers to replace humans, that doesn't make it likely.

As humans, I don't believe we'll allow our own technology to surpass us. Our collective ego is too big. Our pride is too great. Instead, we'll simply **merge** with our technology. Think about it. What's more powerful? Advanced technology or humans in possession of advanced technology?

I think the answer is clear.

WHEN HUMANS MERGE WITH TECHNOLOGY

So what do I mean when I say humans will merge with technology? What I mean is, in an effort to improve themselves, people will use advanced technology to modify their bodies. This isn't something futuristic. It's been happening for a while. For example, an athlete might take steroids or other performance enhancing drugs in an effort to gain an advantage. In a similar way, a person in the future might choose to implant a computer in his brain to increase his intelligence.

Think I'm nuts? I understand why you might feel that way. But look around. We're already in the initial stages, and we have been for a long time. Pacemakers are a prime example. Is a pacemaker "natural"? No. It's a technology people use to improve their health. Artificial heart valves and prosthetic limbs are similar examples. Think those are "natural"? Obviously, they're not. But if necessary, 99 out of 100 people reading this wouldn't think twice about using them. Now, I realize these technologies are simply trying to restore a person's natural abilities. What about improvements that aren't medically necessary?

What if you could build a direct connection between your brain and a computer? Would you? Many will. What if you could connect your brain directly to the Internet or a local network? Would you do it? Again, many will. This is what I mean when I say humans will merge with the technology they create. And in all likelihood, this will occur until little distinction exists between "human" and "machine."

Some would joke and say they know quite a few people who have already merged with their smartphones. But remember this: *All good humor has an element of truth.*

In a sense, these people **have** merged with their smartphones. After all, smartphones function only inches from the human brain. Is it really a stretch to believe some people will eventually implant smartphone-type technology in their bodies? Is it ridiculous to believe some people will want an **instant** connection with others? And if people are willing to do that, why not other forms of technology?

People who have pacemakers or artificial limbs have, in a sense, merged with non-biological human technology. As this technology advances, the human race will undertake much more sophisticated enhancements. This will likely include boosting existing brain power as well as connecting brains to the Internet.

Some of the other possibilities? How about new skin that makes you stronger than steel? Would you modify your body if it made you less susceptible to life-threatening trauma? Again, some will. Would you merge your body with a sophisticated artificial intelligence if it made you super-intelligent? Would you connect your brain to the Internet if it gave you super-awareness or access to the minds of others? How about if you could upload your mind and "live forever"? Again, many will.

How about this… What if you could modify your body to become like Superman or one of your other favorite superheroes? Would you? Many will.

THE TRANSHUMANIST MOVEMENT

You can label me "fringe" or "wacko" for raising these questions, but I'm not the only one who thinks this way. A number of people see this coming, and they're actively preparing for it. In fact, many of them are changing the way they live so they'll survive long enough to take part. True believers have modified their diets, exercise routines, and entire lifestyles in an effort to increase the likelihood of enjoying the fruits of new technologies and the singularity.

Calling themselves "singularitarians" and "transhumanists," these people look forward to the singularity with a religious fervor. Many believe it will lead to the emergence of "post-biological humans." These are people who are able to shed their biological bodies and "upgrade their hardware." As a result, the brain power and physical ability of these posthumans will exceed anything a person of today can imagine. The end result? A human race with abilities so far in excess of what we see today, they appear god-like.

Transhumanists believe this will usher in a new era for the human race. One in which limited mortals shed their biological bodies and set out to conquer the universe. They focus their lives on the continued advance of technology and the promises ahead.

Those promises include extended life, an end to disease and poverty, more leisure time, routine space travel, and an end to the aging process. Many within the transhumanist movement believe advanced technology will also bring about human "immortality." They foresee a day when humans will download themselves onto a computer network, effectively making themselves "immortal" (or so they think).

Once that happens, will we be able to tell the difference between humans and advanced computers? And if not, what are the implications? Will you need a body anymore?

No. You won't need a body anymore. In fact, this is one of the things transhumanists look forward to the most. After all, a flesh and bones body is lanky, awkward, and inefficient. Why wouldn't you look forward to the day when you can "break free" from its biological limitations? Sounds reasonable, right? After all, our bodies get sick. They break. We groan under the labor of the tasks we have to do. If we can cast off these burdens, why not? Many will have no objection to trading in their God-given body for an "upgrade."

And when they do, it's easy to see where all this will lead. That's right. Just like an old VCR or the horse and buggy, flesh and bones will become obsolete.

No "Flesh" Will Survive

If this is true, then one particular passage in the Bible demands our attention. When the disciples met with Jesus on the Mount of Olives and asked Him to describe the signs of His coming and the end of the age, Jesus told them what to look for. Then He said, "Unless those days are shortened, no flesh will survive" (***Matthew 24:22***).

What did Jesus mean when He said this? The traditional interpretation is this… Humanity will bring itself to the brink of destruction in a cataclysmic world war. Then the world will avoid total destruction when Jesus suddenly appears and stops the madness.

But is this what the Bible says? No. The Bible tells us the true reason for Armageddon, and it's not nuclear war, comets, asteroids, or any other Hollywood produced end-of-the-world story. Armageddon is the armies of the world gathering to attack Jesus – the Lord of Heaven's Armies (***Revelation 19:19***).

To do this, people in the end times will have to be much more powerful than the people of past generations. And they will be. They'll be proud and arrogant. "Nothing will be impossible for them" (***Genesis 11:6***). Could it be that in a quest for immortality, they'll shed their fragile flesh and bone bodies in exchange for new ones?

Remember, Jesus didn't say, "Unless those days are shortened, ***no one*** will survive." He said, "***No flesh*** will survive" (***Matthew 24:22***). The key word in this passage is the Greek word "sarx." It doesn't mean "people." It means "flesh" or "animal meat." It refers to the external body, and not necessarily an entire body with a soul. So taken in its original context, it's more accurate to say "no flesh will survive" than to say "no one" or "no people will survive."

Think this is just semantics? Maybe. But what if transhumanists succeed in their quest to create a race of "posthumans" who no longer need human bodies to survive? If that happens, the words of Jesus take on a whole new meaning.

Does all this sound like fantasy? I admit it's hard to accept the idea of humans creating new bodies. It sounds like science fiction. And it's hard to imagine this is what Jesus meant when He said, "no flesh will survive." But our thoughts are limited. They are not God's thoughts (***Isaiah 55:8-9***). Remember, Daniel was given a vision of the end times. What he saw didn't resemble the ancient world in any way. He openly stated he couldn't understand what he had seen (***Daniel 8:15***). Why should it be any different for you and me?

THE RISE OF SUPER HUMANS

Bones break and flesh tears. That's why people wear helmets, and why cars have airbags. Your body is fragile, and blunt trauma to one of your vital organs can lead to a quick and unexpected death. Even if you manage to avoid car accidents and bar fights, your body will eventually grow old. It will decay, and your life will come to an end.

But as humans continue to merge with advanced technology, they'll push to "break free" of the biological limitations of their bodies. When they do, the days of flesh and bones will be over. Most people will opt for modified bodies to better protect themselves. Others will choose to download their brains to the cloud and "live forever" on the Internet – believing they'll always have a "back-up copy" of themselves in case something happens to the original.

In such a world, most people will embrace the transhumanist ideal – to shed their biological bodies and grow in power beyond what most people today believe is possible. Does this sound ridiculous? Perhaps. But it's really not. After all, the Bible says the kings of the earth will plot a war against God Himself. For that to happen, humanity will have to undergo a radical transformation. Is it possible this is what God meant when He made the Tower of Babel prophecy? That left alone, human beings will become so powerful "nothing will be impossible for them?"

It could be. The arrogant desire already lives in our hearts. Most of us already believe our word is superior to God's Word. All that remains is the need for a dramatic increase in human power. An increase that deludes humanity into believing it can overcome the Great I AM. And you know what? Humanity is on the cusp of achieving that power.

CHAPTER 6

Mind Over Matter

MANY YEARS AGO a book profoundly changed my view of the world. The book was first published in 1986 under the title *Engines of Creation: The Coming Era of Nanotechnology*. It has since been updated under the title *Engines of Creation 2.0,* and it's available online as a free ebook. I encourage you to read it.

What makes this book so noteworthy? In *Engines of Creation*, author Eric Drexler describes a future dominated by a revolutionary technology. This technology promises to significantly transform the world. In fact, it's so powerful, every technology developed so far pales in comparison to this future breakthrough. While the words and phrases used to describe it have varied over the years, I believe one in particular offers the best description – molecular manufacturing.

MOLECULAR MANUFACTURING

Imagine for a moment you have the ability to move and "stack" atoms the same way you move and stack a set of blocks. You pick up an atom, and you move it from here to there. In simple terms, that's the promise of molecular manufacturing. And while it's not quite that simple, the idea we'll one day control the basic building blocks of nature on a mass scale is very real. It's far from science fiction. Still find it hard to visualize?

Imagine for a moment something similar to the tip of a fine ink pen. Only this tip is much, much smaller. So small, in fact, its length is measured in terms of atoms instead of inches.

Now, imagine this device uses its "tip" to attract and repel molecules. They either cling to it or fall away from it. For example, using a weak chemical bond, such a device can hold a molecule on its "tip." It could then move that molecule to another place where a stronger chemical bond is formed. Performed correctly, the weak bond will break and the molecule will attach itself to the stronger bond. This is similar to a powerful magnet pulling a metal object away from a weaker magnet. And this process positions those atoms ***perfectly*** to create different shapes.

Think this is nothing more than a daydream? It's not. After all, we're not talking about anything new here. Just basic chemistry. It's nothing more than the breaking and forming of chemical bonds. And that happens all the time in the natural world. But what *is* new is the idea we can control the process from the bottom up instead of the top down. Once we can control this process on a mass scale, everything changes.

Explosive Growth

By itself, such a device is probably nothing more than a novelty. But once it's developed, it can be used to build a second device. Then those two devices can build four more, and so on. That means the creation of a single device will quickly lead to the creation of many more. Line them up, program them with a common purpose, and you end up with a "nanofactory" – a network of these devices working in tandem. Again, this is a simplified explanation. For a more in-depth explanation, I encourage you to explore the work of Eric Drexler and others in his field. However, I think this explanation helps to visualize the concept. Once built, a nanofactory is capable of building almost any physical object with atomic precision.

If you can imagine the scale at which all of this will operate, you'll see a nanofactory is not much different from a traditional factory. When we think of factories and manufacturing today, we tend to think of conveyor belts, gears, and robotic arms. Each is part of a process taking raw materials down an assembly line and transforming them into a finished product. In many ways, this is how a nanofactory will work, only the "factory parts" will be much, much smaller.

Now, this may not seem like such a big deal – moving a molecule from one place to another. Or bonding one molecule to another. But once nanofactories are developed, they'll become a low-cost and powerful means for controlling matter. They'll result in a nearly limitless number of inexpensive products. And the flexibility, durability, and power of those products will far surpass the best of today's technological wonders. In short, once we develop nanofactories, mankind will appear to have complete mastery over the physical universe.

ARE NANOFACTORIES POSSIBLE?

"Sounds good," you might say. *"But is this even possible?"* That's a good question. A lot of smart people claim it isn't. For instance, the late Richard Smalley, Rice University professor and winner of the Nobel Prize in Chemistry, was a champion of nanotechnology. But he was a vocal critic of nanofactories. He believed they would never work in the real world. Yet despite all his accolades, Richard Smalley was (and is) wrong. How can I be so sure?

Because nanofactories already work. That's right. They already exist, and they've existed since the dawn of creation. Think about it. Bacteria, seeds, and humans all provide us with clear proof nanofactories work. In essence, life itself is made up of tiny molecular machines. And every day, those machines use nanofactories.

For example, if you break a bone, your body eventually repairs itself, right? How? Does it need you to apply glue to the broken bone? No. Of course not. It doesn't need glue, tape, or nails. Instead, it uses molecular machines. They may be **biological**, but they're machines nonetheless.

Think about the last time you cut your arm. What did it do? Again, it fixed itself. Sure, maybe you put a Band-Aid or some ointment on it. But you didn't have to. Given a few days, the platelets, proteins, white blood cells, and red blood cells in your body (all of them naturally occurring molecular machines) moved into action. In time, they repaired the gash. No conscious action or heavy lifting was required on your part. After a couple days, the cut disappeared. New skin replaced old, and a week later, no one could tell you ever had a cut on your arm.

Now, compare that process to traditional manufacturing. Assume you accidentally drop your smartphone and the glass display shatters. If you give it some time, will it repair itself? Of course not (at least not at the time this book was written). Since it won't repair itself, you'll need to buy a new display to

Chapter 6

replace the old one. Once you get the new display, you'll need to use tools to remove the old one and get the new one into place.

This shows the sharp contrast between a world of nanofactories and a world of traditional manufacturing. Traditional manufacturing uses a "bulk," top-to-bottom approach. This approach requires you to break larger objects into smaller objects. Then you have to hammer, nail, glue, weld, or fasten those pieces together to create a product. But nanofactories are different. They build from the bottom up – one molecule at a time, adding layer after layer until the product is finished.

This is how the cut on your arm healed. You didn't have to hammer, tape, glue, or weld new skin to your arm. Instead, your body produced new skin tissue one layer at a time. With little fanfare, it simply fixed itself.

At first glance, nanofactories may seem like science fiction. But simple observation of nature proves they're possible. As mentioned, they already surround us (we just don't control them yet). But that day is coming. Because computer models reveal **human-controlled** nanofactories are also possible.

How The World Will Change

Once we develop software giving us the same control over the physical world we have over the virtual world, almost nothing will be impossible. Can you see now why so many people look forward to the coming era of nanofactories?

If you still find it hard to envision, let's think ahead to what the world will be like. Nanofactories will result in a revolutionary product – the **personal** nanofactory. In the not too distant future, every home in the world will have its own nanofactory. This will be a desktop appliance able to create everyday products from basic materials (these materials might take the form of a cartridge of molecules similar to ink cartridges for a printer). Your personal nanofactory will be small, portable, and fully-automated. Using a supply of basic materials, it will assemble molecules into consumer products.

No longer will you have to go to a store and buy those products. You won't even need to have them shipped to your house. You can just **download** them. That's right. In the same way you download songs, ebooks, or apps, you'll be able to download physical objects at home. An entire industry will crop up to provide "apps" for this new capability.

In fact, we already see something similar to this with 3D printing (if you're unfamiliar with 3D printing, look it up on YouTube). 3D printing is itself a revolutionary technology, but it's not a nanofactory. Nor is it anywhere near as powerful. However, it's a close illustration of what's coming.

Imagine this. You log onto the Internet to get a Fisher-Price toy for your two-year-old nephew's birthday. You search the web and find just what you're looking for. You add it to your shopping cart, but instead of the shipping option, you choose the download option. It takes a second or two for the download, and then your nanofactory moves into action.

A short time later, you have all of the toy parts, along with the assembly instructions, just as if you had received them in a box you bought at the local bricks-and-mortar toy store. You snap a few pieces together, and presto! Your toy is ready.

Think about the impact of this scenario. All Fisher-Price had to supply was the design. They didn't have to line up parts distributors or manufacturing partners. They didn't have to guess what consumer demand might be and risk overproducing toy units. They didn't have to ship thousands of toy units from China or stock them on store shelves, and they didn't have to pay UPS or FedEx to ship anything to your door. You built it yourself – and for a fraction of the price you used to pay.

The same product that cost you $50 ten years earlier can now be downloaded for $4.99. And basic designs for common products are available everywhere free of charge. All you pay for are the basic materials feeding your nanofactory. The same way you now pay for ink for your printer.

Does this sound revolutionary? It is. The cost to operate a nanofactory will be relatively small, and nanofactories will be far more efficient and powerful than the factories of the Industrial Revolution. A nanofactory could produce all your daily needs. And it doesn't require large tracts of real estate, high-wage employees, high amounts of energy, expensive equipment, or most of the costs associated with a traditional factory.

And because nanofactories operate with atomic precision, their products will be nearly flawless. They'll have an error rate much closer to zero than today's manufacturing facilities. What does this mean? It means not only will basic products cost a fraction of what they do today, they'll be of higher quality. They'll be less likely to break. More likely to work. And much stronger than today's products.

Compare that with today. Manufacturing a product today requires research, design, raw materials, labor, facilities, equipment, transportation, storage, and sales in order to get from the inventor to the customer. Nanofactories will do away with the need for labor, facilities, equipment, transportation, and storage. The result? A decrease in the price of almost everything.

But nanofactories will be different for another reason as well. And this is what separates them from other breakthrough technologies. A nanofactory will be able to produce a copy of itself. Think about that for a moment. A nanofactory isn't limited to making toys. It can be used to make a second nanofactory. And that capability alone will turn the world upside down.

Exponential Growth

In the Disney version of *Aladdin*, a peasant boy gets three wishes from a genie. But the genie's offer comes with a few rules. One of those rules is "no wishing for more wishes." Makes sense, doesn't it? After all, if you had a magic genie offering you three wishes, you could wish for more wishes. And if he kept granting you wishes, you'd end up with an unlimited number of wishes. Of course, *Aladdin* is a movie. It's not real life. Or is it?

In many ways, nanofactories will be a lot like the magic genie in *Aladdin*. At least with one major difference. **Nanofactories aren't constrained by the magic genie's rule.** One can be used to create another, and those two can create four. And those four can become eight, then sixteen, thirty-two, sixty-four, and on and on. Can you see why this will change the world?

Nanofactories are much more than another technology with an exponential growth pattern. They're the launching pad for a Second Industrial Revolution. When nanofactories emerge, almost everyone on earth will gain access to their own personal wish-granting genie. Does this sound like a dream? Or more like a nightmare?

The Dream Scenario

In many ways, a world with nanofactories will be a dream come true. We'll move from a world of scarcity to a world of abundance. How? Because the basic building blocks needed to produce the world's goods are everywhere. Atoms and molecules are all around us. These raw materials will combine with the power of desktop nanofactories, computer software, solar power, and the

Internet. The result will be an avalanche of inexpensive, high-quality products. Just as today's software, music, and book downloads are sold at a fraction of the cost of those sold in bricks-and-mortar retail stores, you'll be able to download physical goods at a fraction of today's cost. The standard of living for everyone on the planet will skyrocket.

Part of the reason things will become so cheap and abundant is because nanofactories will radically increase the power of existing technologies. For example, energy is one of the highest costs of traditional manufacturing. But nanofactories will run on cheap energy - energy as plentiful as sunlight. Because nanofactories will eliminate much of the cost built into today's consumer products, the cost of living will dramatically ***decrease***. This will free many people from the need to work. For much of the world, it will mean freedom from the burden of manual labor. It will mean a new life. A life spent on creative pursuits and leisure time.

Almost everything will increase in quality and decrease in cost. As this book is written, an estimated 80% of the world lives in poverty. In a world of nanofactories, there's no reason it can't be zero. Here are just a few of the benefits:

Clean, Renewable, and Inexpensive Energy - Believe it or not, an endless supply of cheap energy already surrounds us. In fact, it's so cheap, it's nearly free. What is this energy source? Sunlight. That's right. All the energy we consume today is readily available from the sun. We just need to collect it. As of this writing, we can only capture a small portion, and it's not always the most efficient source of energy. But nanofactories will change that. Nanofactories will construct new materials.

These new materials will require less surface area for collection. They'll also enable us to create better solar batteries. These batteries will store enough power to keep the lights on at night and on cloudy days. When this happens, solar power will become the cheapest and most efficient source of energy on earth. This endless supply of energy will then further fuel the world's nanofactories, continuing the exponential advance of technology.

Increased Health and Wellness - In the near future, people all over the world will enjoy increased health and wellness. Nanofactories will provide better environmental conditions, better food, better diagnostics, and better medical

Chapter 6

treatment. The healthcare of the wealthiest people alive today will seem Stone Age in comparison.

One reason will be a clean water supply. Waterborne diseases kill 3.4 million people every year. But the rise of nanofactories will supply the world with first-rate water purification systems wherever they're needed. Imagine filters with nanoscale pores. Pores so small they're able to sift out all bacteria and viruses. Would you like that? I would. Such filters will give us the closest thing to pure drinking water we've ever had. And because nanofactories will make these filters so cheap and plentiful, clean drinking water won't be reserved for the select few. It will be available for ***everyone***. In such a world, water-borne illness will become a thing of the past.

But water filters aren't the only cheap and plentiful benefits. Nanofactories will make medical supplies cheap and plentiful too. The lower cost and flexibility will provide easy access to the poor. For example, it's not possible to carry every medical tool you might need to the top of Mt. Everest or to a remote village. But with a nanofactory, you'll be able to "print" what you need on the spot. If you need a specific diagnostic test, designer antibiotic, or surgical tool, you can create it in real time. This will do away with the need to store almost any item.

With 3-D printing, we already see this on construction sites. If a highly specialized component breaks in the field, you can create a new one then and there. No need for a costly spare parts warehouse. No need to order the part and wait for days or weeks. This goes for medical supplies as well. You'll be able to manufacture what you need when and where you need it.

And medical treatment? Imagine man-made machines so small they travel through the blood stream. As they encounter deadly bacteria and viruses, they latch on and disable them, effectively ending illness and disease. These designer drugs will attack cancer cells and create healthy ones. Newly designed antibodies will seek out and destroy once deadly viruses. The result? An end to all disease.

Nanofactories will also give us better food. Right now, organic and fresh food is expensive. Nanofactories will drive the cost down, making healthier foods more affordable and more widely available. New designer foods will appear too. When we can put every atom in its place, I'm sure demand will skyrocket for vitamins that taste like chocolate!

Material Abundance – Nanofactories will eliminate the need for expensive production. They won't require huge factories. They won't use high-paid labor. They won't need expensive energy inputs. And you can consume nanofactory products right where they're made. No need for transportation and distribution. Using free sunlight and low-cost materials, nanofactories will create a deluge of low-cost, high-quality products. The result? Material wealth beyond our wildest dreams.

Food will be abundant. Using multi-level greenhouses, food production will multiply. Some of these greenhouses will even be located underground. They'll significantly reduce the surface area needed to grow food. And they'll result in a massive increase in the area available for growing crops. This increase in capacity will result in plummeting food prices.

Remember when we discussed the elimination of labor, facilities, equipment, transportation, and storage? Think of the impact nanofactories will have on housing construction. Building a house will take fewer workers. They could make pre-fabricated parts on site. In such a world, only government regulation could keep the cost of housing from plummeting. Affordable shelter will be available for everyone.

The spread of nanofactories will close the wealth gap between developed and developing nations. In fact, it's unlikely any countries will remain "Third World." The widespread availability of inexpensive supercomputers, digital devices, and high-speed connectivity will bring millions into the modern world. Breakthroughs in solar energy will end the need for high-cost power grid infrastructure. Power will be available anywhere, anytime – independent of the grid. This will allow the poorest nations to transition to wealth far more quickly than they otherwise could.

In a short time frame, hundreds of millions of people will go from lives of poverty and illiteracy to lives of prosperity and learning. This will jump start the invention of new technologies and spark breakthrough discoveries as millions of brilliant minds and productive workers are connected with the rest of the world.

At first glance, all this appears to be a dream come true. A science fiction utopia. Imagine – products built to perfection. Lower repair costs. Fewer broken parts. Higher standards of living. An end to all disease. Plenty of food, water, and shelter for everyone. Is this too good to be true? Unfortunately, it may be. Nanofactories promise immense benefits, but they also have a dark side. And that dark side threatens to turn a dream world into a nightmare.

Chapter 6

NIGHTMARE SCENARIOS

Nanofactories promise a wealth of benefits, but those benefits come with a price. The price is a number of potentially negative impacts. And, no doubt, we have yet to imagine many of them. Does this mean we should avoid nanofactories and advanced technology? No. But it does mean we should prepare for some serious pain.

Consider the Industrial Revolution. Few will argue it was bad. But it also brought social and economic turmoil. Despite its benefits, it led to times of great economic pain and human suffering. Sweatshops, big city tenements, and child labor abuses. It also played a pivotal role in the rise of communism and made the Nazi death factories possible. If the impacts of nanofactories and advanced technology are comparable to the Industrial Revolution, what will be the unintended consequences? Keep in mind, the time frame will be much shorter. The Industrial Revolution took place over two centuries. Imagine similar change jammed into ten years. That's what we face in a world of nanofactories.

So what are the other downsides? Over the years, many people have warned about the nightmare scenarios we could face. Below are just a few:

New Forms of Pollution - Will nanofactories pose a threat to the environment? Some people believe they will. What happens when trash can be measured in nanometers? Will such debris pollute the oceans, our soil, or our drinking water? Will nanoparticles seep into our skin or lungs and make us sick?

These are serious questions. Unfortunately, we probably won't know the answers until nanofactories become a reality. That said, I believe nanofactories will reduce and maybe even eliminate pollution. Why? Because every atom will be in its place, we won't have wasteful byproducts. We'll have better products and better processes for producing them. The pollution of Industrial Age manufacturing will disappear.

And today's trash and landfills? They'll be a great source of basic materials for desktop nanofactories. Many people might keep "home recycling nanofactories." Instead of putting a recycle bin on the curb for weekly trash collection, they'll recycle products in their own home.

While many see stray nanoparticles as a potential environmental concern, I don't think they'll be a problem either. Why? First, they won't be widespread. Products and processes will be better and people will have a financial incentive to recycle, so widespread nanoparticle pollution is unlikely. But let's assume it does become a problem. I'm still not concerned. Why? Because a bunch of smart and conscientious people will devote themselves to cleaning up the environment. And nanofactories will give them powerful tools to make a clean environment reality.

Government Abuse - From a more sinister angle, what if the elites of society decide to kill off the poor? In an automated society of abundance, the need for manual labor will be low. Millions of jobs will disappear. This will likely result in a vastly expanded welfare state. If this happens, the gap between the rich and poor will become even greater. Fear of revolution or a disdain for subsidizing "laziness" might lead the rich to get rid of "the lower classes." As time goes by, what if the elites begin to see themselves as a superhuman master race? They may view the lower classes as a drain on valuable resources. This isn't as absurd as it first sounds. It's how Hitler viewed the mentally disabled, the handicapped, and anyone else he deemed an undesirable drain on the state.

Even if such a division doesn't materialize, nanofactories will give governments access to unprecedented power. For the first time in human history, a surveillance state similar to Orwell's *1984* would be possible. If so, individual privacy could disappear. Will government be able to restrain itself? If not, how will the people protect their individual liberties?

Terrorists with Super Weapons - In an era of nanofactories, immense destructive power will be available to small groups and lone individuals. What if this power is used for mass slaughter? Or even worse, what if the threat of terrorists with super weapons results in the government abuse we just identified? Would governments place *every* citizen under surveillance? They could. In such a scenario, fear of a massive terror attack, coupled with the government's ability to see and know everything, could lead to government abuse and violation of civil liberties.

Chapter 6

WHAT WILL HAPPEN?

At first glance, nanofactories seem like a dream come true. And such devices able to create superior products at a lower cost *are* a dream come true. When every atom is in its place, we'll end up with lighter, stronger, and more durable products.

Humanity could flood the earth with these new products at low cost. We could provide everyone with ample food, shelter, clothing, energy, and access to technology. We would live in a world of overflowing abundance – a world many generations never dreamed possible. Little to no poverty would exist. Little to no pollution. Little to no human suffering from disease and hunger. In fact, nanofactories promise to destroy those evils forever.

But will they?

In my opinion, "No." I'm not so optimistic. Why? Because our problems are *not* material in nature. The rise of nanofactories won't take place in a vacuum. While they will likely result in widespread material abundance, they'll likely do something else as well. It's something every new technology does. Nanofactories will amplify our imperfection. Because no matter how far technology advances, we still live in a fallen world.

Jesus said before His Return the world will experience a time of unprecedented tribulation – the likes of which it has never seen, nor ever will see again. He described it as a time of greater anguish than any other time in human history (*Matthew 24:16-21*). Does this sound terrible? It should.

Just think of the horrors endured in the 20th Century alone. Two world wars. Millions dead from famine. Millions more murdered in the Holocaust. The killing fields of Cambodia. Stalin's pogroms. Yet Jesus says those events don't even compare to what will happen in the years before He returns!

As the singularity approaches, advanced technologies like nanofactories will transform the social, economic, and political power structure of the world. In a short window of time, advanced technology will bring a new era of material abundance never experienced in human history. But at the same time, these new technologies will bring unprecedented global challenges. The world will struggle to deal with new generations of weapons, geopolitical upheaval, and massive economic dislocation.

Global War?

One of those threats – a terrifying global war that kills us all – will command the attention of every world leader. How will the world solve this problem? What can be done to guard against it? How will we avoid total annihilation?

For decades, nuclear war has threatened our existence. Yet such a war hasn't come. Does that mean it will never come? Can we count on this streak of relative peace and stability to continue forever? I don't think so. Why? Again, it's because of the human heart. That's right. The human heart is worse than the most terrible weapons ever devised.

As long as sin infects us, we'll never see peace on earth. But that won't stop the world from chasing it. Once nanofactories arrive, the world will turn to the one option it believes will bring everlasting peace.

And you know what? More than 2,600 years ago, the Bible told us it would come.

CHAPTER 7

The Coming Global Government

LONG AGO, ONE of the most powerful kings in world history faced a dilemma (***Daniel 2:1***). A dream left him deeply disturbed. Unsure of its meaning, he called his advisors and asked them interpret. "Sure," they said. "Tell us your dream, and we'll tell you what it means." But Nebuchadnezzar knew better. He knew if he told them the dream, they could make up its meaning. Would he know if they were right? He wouldn't. So Nebuchadnezzar came up with a foolproof plan. He told his advisors if they were truly wise they would tell him his dream ***and*** its meaning.

Then, he threatened them with death. "Tell me the dream and its meaning," he said. "Or all of you will die." Panicked, they protested. How could anyone know the king's dream? He asked the impossible!

Yet, one man was up to the task. He knew it ***was*** possible. Not because he was a great man. But because Daniel knew, "There is a God in heaven who reveals all things" (***Daniel 2:28***).

After a night of intense prayer, God revealed everything. Daniel described the king's dream. He told Nebuchadnezzar he dreamed of a huge statue of a man. It had a head of gold and a chest and arms made of silver. Its stomach and thighs were bronze. Its legs were iron, and its feet were a mix of iron and clay. In the king's dream, a rock was cut from a mountain. It struck the feet of iron and clay and crushed the whole statue. Then the rock became a great mountain covering the whole earth (***Daniel 2:31-35***).

Daniel then explained the meaning of the dream. The statue was a symbol of successive empires – Babylon, Media-Persia, Greece, and Rome. The rock

Chapter 7

cut from the mountain was Jesus and His everlasting kingdom. According to the dream, Media-Persia would defeat Babylon. Greece would defeat Media-Persia. And Rome would defeat Greece. Then a new form of the Roman Empire would arise. This final empire will rule the world until Jesus destroys it at Armageddon (***Daniel 2:39-45***).

The Coming World Empire

According to Daniel, the Roman Empire will reappear. That's right. Even though the Visigoths sacked Rome in A.D. 410. And even though the Ottomans conquered Constantinople in A.D. 1453, the Roman Empire will return. When it does, it will arrive in the form of a ten nation alliance. These ten nations will join together to strengthen themselves. But they'll struggle to stay together. Daniel compared them to iron and clay, saying some will be as strong as iron while others will be as weak as clay. He also said their alliance will be volatile and unstable (***Daniel 2:43***). Nevertheless, they'll grow into a powerful empire. This new Roman Empire will be so powerful, it will devour the whole world (***Daniel 7:23***).

This means a global empire will one day rule the earth. And when it does, the Bible says the world will be on the brink of Armageddon and the Second Coming of Jesus Christ.

Now, I can understand if you think this means these events are many, many years in the future. After all, as of this writing, the world doesn't seem anywhere close to global government. So you might wonder, *"Why should I care? Even if this happens, it probably won't happen in my lifetime."*

You should care because things aren't always what they seem. In fact, I believe we're on the threshold of global government **right now**. The global empire prophesied in the Bible will be a reality in our expected lifetime. Why do I say this? Because nanofactories and other advanced technologies will transform the current world order. They'll come with several unavoidable consequences. One of them is global government.

The Current World Order

In 1949, the Soviet Union became the world's second nuclear power. Since then, fear of a global nuclear war has kept humanity from destroying itself. The fear of total destruction, the idea no one can win a war between two nuclear powers, is known as Mutual Assured Destruction (MAD). For decades, it's all that's kept us from World War III.

World leaders are well aware – in an all-out nuclear war, no one wins. It's a lose-lose proposition. Because of this, we haven't seen an all-out war between two or more nuclear powers. Many believe we never will. Sure, a regional power such as North Korea or Iran might one day cause a lot of destruction. But could they destroy the entire world? No. But a war between the United States, Russia, or China? That's a different story. For that reason alone, many believe we'll never see them go to war. It makes sense, and in the current era, it may prove true. But just because it's true ***now***, does that mean it will ***always*** be true? No. Why? Because a day is soon coming when MAD will be obsolete.

The End of Mutual Assured Destruction (MAD)

To believe MAD will always rule the day, to believe the threat of nuclear annihilation will forever prevent a war between superpowers, is to believe nuclear weapons are the pinnacle of all technology. They're not. If the past is any indication, something new will replace nuclear weapons. Firearms once made arrows obsolete. Tanks once made horse mounted troops obsolete. And one day soon, new technologies will make nuclear weapons obsolete. When that day comes, MAD will also be obsolete. And that means the world peace built on MAD will fall apart. Why? Because the threat of certain and total destruction will be gone forever.

When post-MAD technologies emerge, decades of world stability will disappear overnight. The old rules will no longer apply. Let's look at what will change:

Defense Against Nuclear Weapons – For much of the nuclear age, there's been little to no defense against nuclear weapons. Once a nuclear weapon is launched, a targeted nation can do nothing to stop it. But that's changing. Missile defense has improved drastically in recent years. New technologies will allow for better tracking of nuclear weapons (preventing the smuggling of nuclear weapons into enemy territory). More importantly, new technologies open up the possibility of disabling nuclear weapons **before** they're launched or detonated. Artificial intelligence, quantum computing, and molecular manufacturing will enable the infiltration of an enemy's closed computer networks and mechanical systems. New technologies could cut off all enemy communications. They could shut down national power grids. In such a world, a nation using outdated nuclear age technology will become just as defenseless as an army with spears trying to fight an army with firearms. Nuclear weapons alone will no longer deter an attack.

A nation with nanofactories could rapidly deploy billions of low-cost machines (both small and large). These machines could have a wide range of capabilities – capabilities we've long thought impossible. Imagine machines able to comb the oceans in search of enemy submarines. Better yet, imagine machines which can **disable** those nuclear subs. Now, imagine similar acts of sabotage against land-based and space-based nuclear facilities and conventional military forces. A nation with post-MAD technologies will be able to perform those feats – feats that seem like science fiction today. In a matter of hours, if not minutes, such a nation could overpower its enemies. They'll be utterly defenseless. This means a nation with nanofactories could conquer at will without fear of nuclear retaliation.

The Unknown – In a world of such technologies, a nation will never be certain of its enemy's capabilities. New breakthrough technologies will emerge quickly. Advances will take place rapidly, and they won't be easy to monitor. And think of this. What if nations put artificial intelligence systems in charge of weapons systems? What if they hand over battlefield command decisions to machine intelligence? Could a non-human decision spark World War III? All this will make the world unstable and unpredictable.

Contributing to this instability will be the ease with which nations can hide their post-MAD weapons programs. Today, not every nation has the ability to develop nuclear weapons. Nuclear development programs are difficult to conceal. But new advanced technology programs will cost less and be harder to track. They'll be easier to conceal. This makes the spread of these technologies much more likely. Even worse, in an age of cyberwarfare, you may not even know **who** your enemy is.

Along the same lines, what if an enemy nation hacks into your weapons systems? In an age of unmanned networked drones, could a hacker turn your own military against you? All these unknowns will create suspicion and instability. And they increase the likelihood of a catastrophic war.

Targeted Destruction – Once the threat of nuclear war is removed, you could once again live in conquered territory. Think about it. After an all-out nuclear war, who would want to live? Few people. What sense does it make to destroy your enemy only to live in a radioactive world?

But new technologies will change this calculation too. If one nation has advanced technologies, and the other doesn't, the former could easily disable the latter. Once its enemies are defenseless, it could conquer at will without fear of nuclear retaliation.

Decreased Economic Cooperation – Advanced technologies will reduce world trade, lessening the impact of war. For example, China and the United States are major trading partners. A war today would devastate each nation's economy. This makes them less likely to go to war. The price is just too high. But what happens when advanced technologies make every nation self-sufficient? When that happens, a major deterrent to war will disappear.

A New Threat

When MAD becomes obsolete, it will end the threat of nuclear war forever. But this isn't necessarily a good thing. Why? Because a new threat will take the place of nuclear war. That new threat is an arms race between nations with post-MAD weapons. Such an arms race will be highly unstable. When it erupts into war, it will destroy the entire world. So while the threat of nuclear war will end, the threat of global destruction will not. In fact, the odds of global destruction will increase.

Doesn't sound like a promising future, does it? But don't worry. As terrible as all this sounds, many people claim they already have the solution.

Chapter 7

GLOBAL GOVERNMENT

What's the solution? Well, think of this. What if Germany had been the first nation to develop the atomic bomb? No doubt Hitler would've used the bomb to drive the Allied Forces from Europe. With enough bombs, he could have totally defeated the United States, England, and Russia. The Third Reich would have dominated the globe.

On the other hand, the United States **was** the world's first nuclear power. The United States could've used its position to prevent other nations from acquiring nuclear weapons. In fact, the United States could've used its position to create an impregnable world empire. Do you see where I'm going?

In a similar fashion, the first nation with post-MAD technologies will have the option to create its own global empire. With its first mover advantage, it could prevent other nations from developing post-MAD weapons. And with the threat of nuclear war gone forever, the path would be clear to conquer any nation on earth. In fact, the path would be clear to conquer *every* nation on earth. If this happens, the threat of a catastrophic war will disappear forever.

In a post-MAD world, many people will recommend this path. They'll see only two options:

1) An unstable arms race ending in global annihilation, or
2) Global government

Now, some will say there's another option. And there is. The other option is eternal cooperation among friendly nations. But is that realistic? What are the odds of an open global society based on mutual accountability and informed, educated citizens? Not so good. I'll bet on global government. Worse than that, I'll bet on global dictatorship. Faced with global destruction in a post-MAD world, some will see it as the only solution. They'll freely join the new global empire. But those who don't? Those nations will need to be conquered.

WORLD WAR III

It's hard to imagine every nation in the world willingly joining a global government. Most will choose war rather than lose their independence. And these nations won't go down without a fight. This means war will be necessary to set up a global government. And even in a post-MAD world, such a war will be enormously destructive.

It's quite unlikely the first nation with nanofactories will be the only one that tried to develop them. It's safe to say many nations will have their own nanofactory development programs. Since they'll all be working at the same time to achieve this monumental breakthrough, one or more will probably have such weapons shortly after the first nation. While they won't be able to conquer the first nation, they'll still be able to inflict incredible damage. A nuclear power could also inflict incredible damage. If the first nation fails to take out the entire nuclear capability of a nuclear power, one or more of that nation's missiles could strike before it's conquered. In either case, the death toll could rival all 20th Century conflicts combined.

Nevertheless, efforts to resist global government will fail. A nation with today's weapons defending itself against a nation with nanofactories will be like a small band of cavemen armed with rocks and spears trying to defeat a modern army. They won't stand a chance. Even a nation state as small as Singapore or Monaco could quickly build a military force far more powerful than all the current world militaries combined.

Think about how the world will change. During the Cold War, vast nuclear arsenals made the United States and the Soviet Union the world's lone superpowers. Likewise, the first nation with nanofactories will become the world's next dominant superpower. If it uses its advantage to take out its rivals, it could cement its superpower status *forever*.

Is this what the first nation will do? While we'd like to think it's one of many options, reality is different. World domination won't simply be one of many options. It will be the **only** option. Because once MAD is obsolete, allowing a second nation to develop nanofactories and artificial intelligence would be global suicide. The first nation to develop these technologies will see only one viable option – preserving its monopoly and using its power to reshape the world. In short, global empire will be the only option. Think I'm exaggerating? Vladimir Putin doesn't.

In a September 2017 address to Russian students, he said, "the one who becomes the leader in this sphere will be **the ruler of the world**" (emphasis mine). Have no doubt. Putin understands the stakes. A race is on. It's a race to create nanofactories and advanced artificial intelligence. The second place nation gets nothing. The first place nation gets the whole world. I'm sure

Chapter 7

Putin imagines he'll win the race. But regardless of who wins, the leading nation will draw the same conclusion he did – global government is coming.

Think about that. The world is fast approaching a time when global government is certain. It's not a matter of *if*, it's a matter of *when*. This shouldn't surprise anyone. It's exactly what the Bible foretold centuries in advance. Just a coincidence? I don't think so. Without global government, a post-MAD arms race is certain. And such an arms race will destroy the world. So whether it's for noble purposes or selfish reasons, any world leader will gladly choose global empire over global destruction.

GLOBAL GOVERNMENT IN THE END TIMES

The Bible is clear. A global empire will rule the world in the end times. It will be the most powerful empire in world history. It will smash and crush all nations (***Daniel 2:40***) and devour the whole earth (***Daniel 7:23***).

The Book of Revelation says this empire and its ruler (the Antichrist) will have power over every tribe, people, language, and nation (***Revelation 13:7***). No one will escape its grasp. It will be so powerful no one can imagine anyone or anything opposing it (***Revelation 13:4***).

The absolute power of such a state is hard to fathom. But centuries ago, the Bible foretold many other hard-to-imagine events set to take place in the end times. Many of these events once seemed impossible, but not anymore. They include:

- Global government (***Revelation 13:4***)
- One man in total control of the world (***Revelation 13:7***)
- Total economic control of the world (***Revelation 13:16-17***)
- Weapons able to destroy one third of the land (***Revelation 8:7***)
- Weapons able to destroy one third of the sea (***Revelation 8:8***)
- The entire world watching two people (***Revelation 11:9***)

While each of these events *could* have taken place at any time in history, it's much easier to visualize them in a world of advanced technology. In a world of e-commerce, it's easy to imagine government controlling who can buy or sell.

In a world of modern weapons, it's easy to imagine a third of the land and sea on fire. In a world of mobile devices, it's easy to imagine the whole world can watch an event in real time.

More importantly, in a world of nanofactories and artificial intelligence, it's easy to believe one man could control a global empire. One man with power over every person on earth. But if nanofactories play a pivotal role in the end times, shouldn't we expect the Bible to describe what will happen when nanofactories emerge? Yes. We should. Does the Bible do that? Yes. It does. In fact, one of the most quoted phrases in the Bible takes on new meaning in the face of advanced technology. It describes exactly what we would expect to happen once the world develops nanofactories.

The Four Horsemen of the Apocalypse

Even if you've never opened a Bible, I'll bet you've heard the phrase "four horsemen of the apocalypse." These horsemen appear in the Book of Revelation, and they symbolize the first events of the Tribulation. But you know what else? They also offer a perfect description of what will happen in a post-MAD world.

Horseman #1 – The Rider on the White Horse

The first horseman appears in chapter six of the Book of Revelation (**Revelation 6:1-2**). He rides a white horse. He also carries a bow and has a crown on his head. The rider on this horse is the Antichrist, and he goes out to conquer many nations (**Revelation 6:2**). Now, if you read these verses, you'll notice something interesting. The Antichrist carries a bow, but no arrow (**Revelation 6:2**). Because he has a bow but no arrow, this tells us he doesn't use deadly force (at least not in the initial phase of his conquest).

Many believe this is because he'll achieve victory through diplomacy or manipulation. And this could be the case. After all, the Book of Daniel describes the Antichrist as a "master of intrigue" (**Daniel 8:23**) and a "master of deception" (**Daniel 8:25**). Because of this, many bible prophecy experts believe he will peacefully bring a willing world into an era of global government. And maybe he will. But is this the only possibility?

I don't think so. It's unlikely *everyone* in the world will submit to the

Antichrist without a fight. Some might, but not all. Given the history of nationalism, tribalism, racism, and other animosities among men, it's hard to believe any man could conquer the world with mere words. It doesn't matter how charismatic he is.

But even so, how could he conquer a nation without using deadly force? This has been the way of all conquerors throughout history. While it's true Hitler annexed lands around Germany without using force, ultimately it was the ***threat*** of deadly force that allowed him to do so. Is this what the Antichrist will do? Probably not. A warrior with an unloaded weapon isn't very threatening. And Revelation 6:2 tells us the Antichrist will set out to conquer many nations. Could it be he uses ***military*** force to conquer nations, but he doesn't use ***deadly*** force?

No. Right now, that's not possible. But with future technologies? Yes. It is.

If the Antichrist is the first to develop nanofactories, then the first horseman may be a description of a campaign to conquer his rivals and avoid a post-MAD arms race. With nanofactories, the Antichrist ***could*** conquer many nations without using deadly force. With superior technology, he could disable enemy weapons, shut down enemy communications networks, and knock out enemy power systems. Using swarm technology, he could send billions of tiny drones against his enemies.

Imagine swarms of bees, grasshoppers, or locusts. Only these swarms are man-made, stronger than steel, and directed by an enemy. The Antichrist could use these swarms to target a nation's government and military leaders. Rather than killing them, he could simply knock them out. The swarms could sedate his enemies before he takes them into custody. With this type of power, the Antichrist ***could*** bring the world under submission rather quickly and without great bloodshed.

But as any good military strategist will tell you, "No battle plan survives contact with the enemy." No matter how overwhelming the Antichrist's forces may be, any war is going to have unforeseen consequences. The nations he targets aren't likely to give in without a fight. What if some of their conventional forces survive the initial attack? What if nuclear weapons are launched before they're disabled? This is where the second horseman enters the picture.

Horseman #2 – The Rider on the Red Horse

When the Antichrist sets out to build his global empire, he's unlikely to find a willing and compliant world. Many nations will resist. The result will be an event many people have long thought the world could never survive – World War III. But you know what? The world will survive. Because the Bible says World War III is what the second horseman brings.

Sitting atop a red horse, the second horseman has a "mighty sword," and he causes war and slaughter throughout the world (***Revelation 6:4***). Once again, this represents the Antichrist. But what is his "mighty sword?" No one knows. Could it be a post-MAD superweapon? It might. We don't know for sure. But we do know one thing. This mighty sword is a unique and powerful weapon. No other "mighty swords" are mentioned in these verses. And why mention his "mighty sword" if it's just one of many?

Does this verse support the idea the Antichrist will be armed with nanofactories and post-MAD superweapons? Again, while we can't be sure what the "mighty sword" is, it opens the possibility.

If the Antichrist is the first world leader with a nanofactory, he'll understand global government is the only way to avoid an unstable post-MAD arms race. What if he stops other nations from developing their own nanofactories? What if he claims the only way to save the world is to conquer it? If he did, wouldn't you expect global events to unfold in the same way the Bible depicts?

If the Antichrist sets out to conquer the world with post-MAD weapons, he'll have clear military superiority. The weakest nations will fall first. But nations with their own nanofactories, post-MAD weapons, and even nuclear weapons will pose a greater challenge. Defeating them will be bloody. The amount of destruction? Catastrophic.

The resisting nations may experience an isolated victory or two. But they won't win. An advantage of just a few months (or maybe as little as a few weeks) will provide the Antichrist with an insurmountable advantage. Why? Because the power of technology increases exponentially.

If one nation is just a few months behind in developing nanofactories, they won't be able to catch up. They won't have the firepower to compete. Think about European colonization of the New World. European explorers fought with gunpowder and the most advanced weapons of their day. Local natives fought with arrows and spears. Even though they outnumbered the

Europeans, is anyone surprised the Europeans won? No. Of course not. Everyone knows they held an overwhelming advantage because of superior technology. The local natives never had a chance.

Nanofactories will provide a similar overwhelming advantage. If you put today's best weapons up against nanofactories and their associated technologies, it will be no different than using arrows and spears against 16th Century firearms. Post-MAD weapons will be hundreds of times stronger, lighter, faster, and more accurate than the best military technologies of today. They'll amplify the current march toward smaller, more precise, and efficient weapons. A nation with nanofactories will have an almost unlimited capacity to produce arms and military equipment. Its weapons will be easy to hide. They'll be difficult to track and destroy. And even if they are destroyed, they could be replaced quickly.

For these reasons, the idea of multiple nations with nanofactories living in peaceful co-existence is wishful thinking. MAD will be obsolete. The rapid development of new technologies and the ability to hide secret programs will create constant instability and paranoia. Nations will view each other with suspicion. Volatility will mark the times. Is it such a stretch to believe these conditions will lead to "war and slaughter everywhere" (**Revelation 6:4**)? No. Especially when the Bible says a global war is coming. And the Bible says it will end with a single victor and a global empire.

Does this mean the arrival of nanofactories and post-MAD weapons is the scenario foreseen in Revelation 6:2-4? Maybe. Maybe not. The Tribulation could occur before these advanced technologies arrive. But if it doesn't, then nanofactories and post-MAD weapons *will* play a role in the fulfillment of Revelation 6:2-4. How can I be so sure? Because nanofactories and post-MAD weapons will bring about the same scenario, and the end result will be a global empire – just as the Bible says.

Also, keep this in mind. Many believe nanofactories and post-MAD weapons will appear in the near future – in our expected lifetime. When you realize ours is the only generation to see all the signs Jesus and the prophets said to look for, you have a recipe for the fulfillment of end times bible prophecy.

Mere coincidence? Could be. But it could also be a sign of things to come.

RULING THE WORLD

While most people believe the next world war will end all life on earth, remember this – conventional wisdom is often wrong. The Bible says a global war (***Revelation 6:4***) will one day result in one world government (***Revelation 13:7***). Such an empire will be a first in human history. After all, as powerful as it was, the ancient Roman Empire never came close to true global domination. No empire has.

Not only did Rome fail to rule the entire world, its leaders didn't even know whole continents existed. Even if they could have conquered the whole world, how would they have ruled it? First century global government would have been a bureaucratic nightmare. Even today, it would prove nearly impossible.

Think I'm wrong? Then consider this. As of this writing, the United States is the most powerful nation on earth. Yet it spent over a decade struggling to govern the relatively small nations of Iraq and Afghanistan. Although the U.S. could have easily destroyed both, creating law and order proved a much tougher task. And that's just Iraq and Afghanistan. Imagine trying to rule and regulate *the entire world*. How would it be possible? It wouldn't, and it isn't. But the Bible says a day is coming when it will be.

And what about the *type* of global rule described in the Bible? No nation or empire has ever approached it. Even with current technology, it's impossible. Why? Because not only would a global government have to rule over every person on the face of the earth, it would have to be so powerful no one could attack it (***Revelation 13:4***). It would have to track every transaction on the planet to make black markets impossible (***Revelation 13:17***). No nation today has that type of power.

Yet some would argue otherwise. They'll point to a state like North Korea and claim they have that type of power. It's true the regimes of Kim Jong-un in North Korea, the Taliban in Afghanistan, and others have succeeded in taking state control to heights never before seen. But none of those nations has the type of power the Bible says the end times global empire will have. Every one of them is home to black markets, secret resistance movements, spies, and other elements of dissent. No society in history has achieved the level of state control the Bible predicts. But the end times global empire will.

How will it achieve this power? Easy. The same way it created a global empire in the first place – advanced technology. With advanced technology, one man can rule the entire world with an iron fist. With advanced technology, one government can control and regulate every aspect of daily life. And with advanced technology, the Antichrist can fulfill the Tower of Babel prophecy – a world with no borders and no language barriers. A united world with one people and one purpose.

For centuries, even the ***thought*** of a global empire as powerful as the one described in the Bible seemed ridiculous. But it's coming. And when it arrives, it will dominate the world. No nation or person will escape its reach. No outside army will threaten it. And no one will be invisible to its watchful eye.

With advanced technology, a global empire like the one described in the Bible won't just be a possibility. It'll be a necessity. The need for global security guarantees it. So what does this mean? It means the coming global empire will track every human being on earth. And to do so, it will see, hear, and record ***everything***.

CHAPTER 8

The Rise of Big Brother

IN HIS FAMOUS book *1984*, George Orwell introduced the concept of "Big Brother" – an omnipresent, all-powerful and "well intentioned" totalitarian regime. The book's hero, Winston Smith, resides in Oceania where every citizen lives under 24/7 surveillance. Personal privacy is non-existent. Government controls every aspect of life. Monitors in Winston's apartment spy on him when he's home. Hidden cameras and microphones capture his words, deeds, and even his facial expressions. His mail is opened, and "thought police" search for and arrest any citizens who dare to have thoughts or feelings unaligned with those of Big Brother and the ruling elite.

Winston's world is a place of absolute government control. No conversation, movement, or transaction goes unnoticed. The government is watching – *always*. In the decades since Orwell first released *1984*, people have marveled at what they see as great insight into our future. They're right to do so. Because, unfortunately, the world of *1984* will one day become reality. How can I be so sure? Because the Bible says a global empire will one day control the world using technology far more powerful than George Orwell's Big Brother.

GLOBAL TOTALITARIAN GOVERNMENT

As stated before, the Bible says a global empire will rule the world (***Daniel 7:23***). No one will escape it. It will reign over every people, tribe, nation, and language (***Revelation 13:7***). It will control every economic transaction. So much so, no one can buy or sell without its permission (***Revelation 13:17***).

Chapter 8

The power of this global empire will be complete and total. And unlike *1984*, rival nations won't exist. No one will wage war against it (**Revelation 13:4**). No foreign army will come to the rescue, because no foreign armies will exist.

But how? How could one government acquire such power? We already answered how and why a global empire will come into existence. But how does it exercise such complete control over the world? How could one government regulate everything that's bought and sold? The answer is simple. The coming global empire will rule the world with the same technology it used to conquer it.

And have no doubt, it will ***rule*** the world. It won't be an empire of unfettered freedom and liberty. It will be an empire of constant surveillance and invasion of privacy. How can I be so sure? One reason – the darkness of the human heart.

THE COMING SURVEILLANCE SOCIETY

Imagine you're standing on a hilltop or the top floor of a building. Off in the distance, you see what looks like dark smoke. A few seconds pass. It rises higher and forms a large cloud on the horizon. Is it a dust storm? No. You quickly realize it's not. It's a swarm of man-made machines the size of tiny insects. In a matter of minutes, they sweep across the land and blanket everything around you. You swat at them, but it's no use. They crawl over, under, and around you. They attack and kill people everywhere.

Is this the future of terrorism? In due time, it will be. Now think of this. What if terrorists unleash these tiny armies on a city like Tokyo? More than 30 million people live in Tokyo. How many will die? The death toll could be staggering. And that's just one city. Other urban areas with millions of people will also be at risk – New York, Seoul, Mexico City, Manila, and on and on. Terrorists could use advanced technology to secretly create such an army. In fact, they could quickly create an army so vast it could threaten the entire world.

This will be an ongoing threat in the post-MAD world. By conquering the world, the leading power will forever end the threat of war between two nations armed with these technologies. But it won't end ***all*** threats to world peace. Terrorism will remain a problem. And not only will it remain a problem, it will become an even bigger problem. Because advanced technology will open the door for terrorists to obtain weapons of unprecedented power.

With nanofactories and their associated technologies, a small group of people could conquer the whole world. A terrorist group could build its own military and challenge the global empire. How will the global empire guard against these threats? The same way the world guards against them now.

Today, intelligence agencies track and infiltrate terrorist camps, hate groups, and enemies of the state. When nanofactories and artificial intelligence appear, it will become much more difficult to track these groups **and** respect personal liberty. Unfortunately, with the stakes so high, freedom and liberty are likely casualties. While terrible, today's terrorists can't destroy the whole world. But tomorrow's terrorists? They'll have such power. Stopping them will be the world's number one priority.

How will they do it? Intelligence gathering will go to a whole new level. The world will turn to 24/7 surveillance. The entire globe will become a surveillance society not unlike Orwell's *1984*.

Think you already live in a "surveillance society"? If so, I can't blame you. Take your smartphone for instance. It sends off signals. Those signals are tracked. Apps use them to reveal traffic patterns. Retailers use them to track the path you take through a store and how long you spend in front of a product display. In fact, your smartphone reveals almost everything about you – your location, your social connections, everything…

Who's on your speed dial? Who are your Facebook friends? Who do you text or call the most or least? Where do you do your banking? Your phone knows all the answers. If you carry your smartphone everywhere you go, then GPS tracks your location everywhere you go. If the government has the information on your phone, it knows almost everything about you.

What about your web surfing habits? Did you know there's a record of everything you do online – *forever*? Every website you've ever visited. Every email you've ever sent. It's all stored. The government can retrieve it all. And it's the same with phone calls and text messages. Voice recognition technologies already scan your phone calls, both landline and mobile. Algorithms already sift through every phone call, email, and text message.

And that's just your digital footprint. What about cameras? Cameras are everywhere. Street corners, store fronts, residential neighborhoods. Inside and outside of buildings. Most of them go unnoticed. And microphones are everywhere too. In televisions, phones, laptops, and other devices. They can and often do listen to what you say.

Chapter 8

There's no escaping it. Nothing is private anymore.

But unfortunately, you haven't seen anything yet. Believe it or not, future technology will make today's surveillance seem Stone Age in comparison. It'll be everywhere. Think it already is? Trust me, it's not. But it's coming. Soon, the government will have access to *everything* you say or do.

How Is This Possible?

It's possible because of the same technologies that will make MAD obsolete. It's possible because of the same technologies that will allow one nation to conquer the world with relative ease. These same technologies will give rise to a new generation of surveillance tools. Think about it. In the past, what kept government from spying on every aspect of human life? The answer is simple. Resources.

No government has ever had the resources. They're just too massive. To bug every possible meeting space, have cameras everywhere, or have government agents in every location has always been too costly. And that's assuming the technology existed to make it possible anyway. But another obstacle has blocked 24/7 surveillance.

Even if you could gather every piece of information – every conversation, every email, every text, and every act a person performs – what would you do with all the information? How would you process that much data? How would you "connect the dots" and make sense of what you've gathered? You couldn't. But that won't be true forever.

Technologies just around the corner will tackle both of these problems. Nanofactories will open the door to an endless supply of cameras and listening devices. Using solar energy and cheap raw materials, a global government could make trillions and trillions of HD cameras and microphones.

You might be thinking, *"Sure, Britt. **Trillions** of cameras and microphones? That's ridiculous. Where would they put so many devices?"* If that's what you're thinking, I get it. But devices of the future won't be like the devices of today. Imagine each one of those trillions of cameras and microphones is the size of a dust particle. Some might be so small the naked eye can't see them. These cameras and microphones will constantly record everything. How will they be placed? They won't. Just like dust, they'll spread across the earth and settle on every surface. They'll be everywhere.

They'll settle on your clothes. They'll come in through the ventilation in your house. They'll stick to the bottom of your shoes, and they'll blow through the streets. They'll be everywhere. And this "nanodust" will send raw video and audio content straight to the government where it's stored forever. How could the government possibly store so much information? Again, advanced technology. Once nanofactories appear, they'll be able to create storage devices far more powerful than those of today. Storage devices so small they can't be seen will be able to hold all the information now available on the Internet.

And how will the government sift through all this data? It would take legions of intelligence analysts a century or more to listen to just one day of global conversations. That's true. But humans won't comb through this data. Computers will. Nanofactories will arrive in tandem with other advanced technologies such as quantum computers and artificial intelligence. Quantum computers will be thousands of times faster than today's fastest computers. As quantum computers process the reams of data coming in every day, artificial intelligence will analyze that information to a much higher level of precision than any human analyst ever could.

With these powerful technologies working together, a global government will have the ability to "listen" to every conversation on earth. You'll have no place to hide. Even if you could manage to clear an area of all "nanodust," the government will know. They'll see their "blindness" to that area and investigate.

Think all of this sounds ridiculous? It's not. Even without these technologies, governments are already moving down this road. Through its PRISM surveillance program, the U.S. National Security Agency (NSA) collects and stores all internet communications. Through the ECHELON program, the United States, Australia, Canada, New Zealand, and the United Kingdom intercept global government, private, and commercial communications. The European Union's INDECT program focuses on the development of systems to process video data streams captured by public cameras. And these are just a few of the many programs we know of. How many more exist?

And what if government surveillance could track your thoughts? Sounds crazy, doesn't it? Only it's not. Neuroengineers are already developing technologies to read a person's inner thoughts. These technologies measure brain activity and use algorithms to interpret patterns. This effectively results in reading a person's mind. The reason for developing this technology is to help people who can't speak. But what happens when this technology is used for evil? What happens if government uses it to read minds? If that happens, even your thoughts won't be private.

In such a world, fugitives will have no place to hide and no way to escape. The government will know where everyone is at any given moment. Everything you do and say will be seen and heard by an all-powerful, omnipresent government. And the one who controls this system will have complete power over the entire world.

UNRIVALED POWER

The Bible clearly says who that person will be. Advanced technology will give the Antichrist unrivaled power. Power so great, no one's ever seen anything like it. He'll control the global surveillance system and dominate the entire world (***Revelation 13:7***).

The Bible says he'll worship a god of fortresses unknown to his forefathers (***Daniel 11:37-39***). His rule will be so complete, people will worship him (***Revelation 13:4***). They won't just obey him. They'll delight in following him. The question is, "Why?" Why will people submit to him? In a world of competing nations and cultures, why will so many people willingly follow the Antichrist? Part of the answer is found in a story more than 4,000 years old. It's a story of crisis, desperation, and growing governmental power.

And like the Tower of Babel story, it's more than just a biblical footnote – it's a prophecy of things to come.

CHAPTER 9

The Great, Great Depression

SOMETIME AROUND 4,000 years ago, the Pharaoh of Egypt summoned an imprisoned slave named Joseph. Two dreams bothered Pharaoh, and none of his magicians or wise men could interpret them (***Genesis 41:1-8***). In his first dream, Pharaoh saw seven fat, healthy cows grazing by the Nile. Then seven thin cows appeared and ate the seven fat ones. In his second dream, Pharaoh saw seven large, beautiful heads of grain. Then seven shriveled heads of grain appeared and swallowed up the first seven.

Pharaoh asked Joseph to interpret the dreams. "I don't have the power to do this," Joseph told him. "But God does, and He can tell you what it means." Joseph went on to tell Pharaoh the meaning of the dreams. He said seven years of famine will follow seven years of plenty.

In response, Pharaoh made Joseph the second most powerful man in Egypt (***Genesis 41:40***). He put him in charge of the land, and Joseph collected one-fifth of the food produced for the next seven years. He stored up massive amounts. When the famine came, it hit neighboring nations hard. People from the lands all around Egypt came to buy grain from Joseph (***Genesis 41:57***).

Eventually, the people ran out of money. They had nothing to buy food. So they gave Joseph their livestock in exchange for food (***Genesis 47:17***). When their livestock was gone, they offered their land and themselves (***Genesis 47:19***). Before long, Pharaoh owned all the land in Egypt (***Genesis 47:20***). The people became his slaves, and Pharaoh's power multiplied.

Most have heard the story of Joseph. But like the Tower of Babel, it's

Chapter 9

more than a Sunday school lesson. Just as Abraham's willingness to sacrifice Isaac foreshadowed Jesus on the cross (**Genesis 22:9-12**), the story of Joseph and Pharaoh foreshadows a coming time of great famine. It also foreshadows a time when, like Pharaoh, one man will gather immense power over the known world.

The seven lean years of Pharaoh's dream mirror the seven year period known as the Tribulation. Like the seven lean years, the Tribulation will begin with widespread famine. And in an effort to survive, people throughout the world will willingly give their power and wealth to one man – just as they gave their power and wealth to Pharaoh four thousand years ago.

The Coming Famine

Famine often follows war, and World War III will be no different. Destruction will be widespread. Supply chains disrupted. People scattered. Famine is what the Bible says will follow the outbreak of global war.

The third horseman in the Book of Revelation represents this coming famine. Riding a black horse, he holds a pair of scales, while a voice calls out "A loaf of wheat bread or three loaves of barley for a day's pay. And don't waste the olive oil and wine" (**Revelation 6:5-6**). What does this mean?

It means a worldwide famine is coming. The rider's scales suggest a need to carefully measure and ration the food supply. We know because the voice that calls out indicates a scarcity of food. Three loaves of barley are about one pint. Many believe this is the minimum amount of food needed to survive. Yet this verse is telling us a time is coming when an entire day's wage will buy just enough food to survive. The reference to "olive oil and wine" represents the rich. When the Book of Revelation was written, olive oil and wine were luxury items. This tells us the famine will not impact the rich the same way it impacts everyone else.

In other words, some will indulge in the luxuries of this world while others scramble to survive. The beginning of the Tribulation will bring scarcity and famine for some, while others enjoy wealth and opulence. So while most people associate the Tribulation with global destruction and misery, the Bible says it will be a time of great prosperity for some (**Revelation 18:12-13**).

Why does this matter? First, it shows why most of the world will willingly give their power to the Antichrist. Just as they did during the famine in ancient Egypt, the world will willingly give everything in exchange for survival. Second, like the rest of Revelation 6, this closely mirrors what many people believe will happen when nanofactories and post-MAD weapons become reality.

The Economic Impact of Advanced Technology

Imagine you're an early 18th Century cobbler. You make shoes by hand. Now, imagine yourself magically transported to the early 21st Century. Does your skill set have any value in the modern world? If not, how will you make a living?

Let's be generous and say there's a market of wealthy people willing to pay a premium for hand-made shoes. You might be back in business. But what if there are two thousand other unemployed cobblers with the same skill set? Is there enough demand for everyone? What if a machine can create shoes completely identical to the hand-made items you make? What if they're better? Will anyone pay *you*? These are the questions that will quickly confront nearly everyone who depends on trading their time or labor to earn a living. Tens of millions (if not hundreds of millions) of jobs will become obsolete. And they'll become obsolete almost overnight.

Why will this happen? Because most jobs can be automated. They haven't yet because it hasn't been cost effective to do so. But that will change soon. Nanofactories will make widespread automation cost effective. Once nanofactories arrive, millions of jobs will disappear.

This will turn the global economy upside down. When the dust settles from World War III, the Antichrist will have a global empire. He'll also have a number of problems to deal with. One of those will be a global famine. And for a short time, nanofactories will compound the global famine by creating mass unemployment.

Remember, a nanofactory can produce two nanofactories at low cost. Those two can produce four, then eight, and so on. In a matter of weeks, the first nanofactory could spawn billions of new ones. The ability to manufacture almost anything at low cost, coupled with the development of artificial intelligence, will lead to the quick automation of millions of jobs. The current global economy will be transformed overnight when faced with this new reality.

Chapter 9

In short, nanofactories will bring economic upheaval unlike anything the world has ever seen. Here are just a few of the impacts:

Driverless Trucks, Cars, and Boats – Already we've seen the first driverless vehicles on the road. Using GPS and computers, self-driving cars are the next big thing in the auto industry. These cars know the traffic laws, never get distracted, and never fall asleep.

Due to incentives, the adoption of driverless technology will come much faster than most people think. Those with driverless cars will get cheaper auto insurance rates. And millions of people will give up owning a car altogether. They'll simply a join a club like Uber or Lyft, pay a flat monthly fee, and use their smartphone to summon a driverless car when they need one.

Trucking companies will look at the cost of paying a salary and benefits to a human driver and make the decision to automate. A fleet of driverless trucks will be far more cost effective. Driverless trucks will operate around the clock. They'll never call in sick. And they'll never fall asleep at the wheel. The hassle of finding and training truck drivers will go away. And driverless trucks will operate at peak efficiency and fuel economy. Why wouldn't trucking companies automate?

They will. The competition will crush them if they don't. Those trucking companies that don't automate won't be in business for long. And don't think driverless technology will be limited to the trucking industry. The same technology will revolutionize shipping as well. Why pay an expensive crew to man a fleet of ships when you can automate the whole process?

Driverless technology will spread quickly. When it does, millions of jobs will disappear overnight. No more truck drivers. No more taxi cab drivers. No more shipping captains.

Automated Manufacturing – Already, automation has taken millions of manufacturing jobs. Yet, tens of millions of people still work in manufacturing facilities throughout the world. That said, it's only a matter of time before most of those jobs disappear too. This shouldn't surprise you. When it comes to humans vs. robots, robots are faster and cheaper. And with each passing day, they get even more faster and even more cheaper. Soon, they'll take almost every factory job in the world.

If those jobs disappear in the span of six months, what will those unemployed workers do? What happens when people can manufacture products in their own homes? What happens when construction workers (or construction robots) can manufacture a tool or part they need on site? Not only will millions lose their manufacturing jobs, but millions will lose their warehouse and delivery jobs as well. Quick, cheap production wherever it's needed will transform manufacturing. Again, it's impossible to foresee the exact impact. Manufacturing is a big space. Some companies may go on a hiring spree. But for workers who perform repetitive tasks or have jobs that don't require creative decision making, it's safe to say their jobs will disappear forever.

Off-Grid Solar Energy – For decades, people have looked forward to the day when solar energy becomes a viable alternative to fossil fuels. Yet it hasn't happened. Solar panels take up too much space. Often the cost of those panels is too high to make up for the fact sunlight is free. And even once you collect sunlight, storing it becomes a problem. How do you use solar energy when it's cloudy for a week? You have to store the energy you collect when it's sunny. And we haven't been able to do that yet. At least, not in a way that's cost effective.

But in a world of nanofactories, solar energy collection will be much more efficient. The cost of solar components will plummet. We'll be able to collect far more sunlight per square inch, *and* we'll be able to store it. The result? Solar energy will power almost every device we use. Cars, phones, households, streetlights. Everything. And this will happen quickly. When it does, what will happen to all the jobs associated with coal and oil production? What about jobs at the local power company? We can't know for sure. But one thing is certain – massive change is coming to the energy industry.

A Collapse in International Trade – What will happen to international trade once nanofactories become reality? Many believe trade between nations will come to a screeching halt, as it will no longer be necessary in most cases. What will ultimately happen remains to be seen. It's likely some markets will continue to thrive, such as handmade Cuban cigars, authentic French wine, and a number of other historically sought after luxury items. However, it's also likely we'll see major disruptions. And what worries many is the reduced interdependence between nations. Yes, nations *can* continue to trade with each other. But they don't *have* to. If a nation wanted to, it could isolate itself and produce everything within its own borders. If that happens, the odds of war increase.

A Massive Debt Crisis – What will happen to those in debt when nanofactories become reality? If millions become unemployed in a matter of months, how will they pay their mortgage, car loan, or student debt? And what will that mean for banks? Think about the 2008-2009 financial crisis. Contagion spread throughout the global system. Remember, one man's debt is another man's asset. If debt can't be paid back, it impacts the entire global economy. If nanofactories bring mass unemployment, expect a financial crisis far worse than any we've ever experienced.

CREATIVE DESTRUCTION

All this sounds a bit alarmist. And it's impossible to know the precise impact on the global economy. Nanofactories won't be rolled out in a single day. But knowledge of their existence will be enough to send shockwaves around the world. They'll leave capital markets in chaos. They'll crush entire industries. The need for much of today's supply chain, including massive factories, transportation networks, and storage facilities will go away.

But hasn't this always happened? Hasn't technology always destroyed jobs? It has. This is nothing new. The process of "creative destruction" is something we've observed for almost three centuries. New technologies and new processes come along and upend the old way of doing things. Companies go bankrupt. People lose jobs. But in the long run, everyone wins.

So if that's the case, what makes this so bad? What makes it so bad is the *speed* of the process. When nanofactories appear, the process of creative destruction will be shoved into a much shorter time frame. Radical change will engulf entire industries much faster than in the past.

While nanofactories will impact every business on the planet, some will experience a death blow. While no one can know for sure what will happen, the following industries are likely to see a dramatic contraction:

- Shipping
- Distribution

- Storage
- Fossil fuels (oil and natural gas)

On the flipside, some industries will see dramatic growth. They likely include:

- Solar energy
- Software
- Intellectual property
- Consumer products
- Prime real estate

While we can't know exactly what impact nanofactories will have on global commerce, we can be certain of one thing. A period of great volatility and uncertainty will follow their arrival. It seems likely they'll cause widespread economic pain in the short-term. Think about it. A sharp drop in international trade. Tens of millions of jobs lost. Personal fortunes destroyed. And a massive contraction in consumer spending. In a world economy built on debt (and a reliance on timely payment of debt), these sudden changes will plunge the world into a global economic meltdown – *for a short time.*

Will such a scenario result in temporary food shortages or skyrocketing food prices? Probably not. But when you combine these economic changes with a global war? That's another story. Will a global war and the greatest economic collapse since the Great Depression lead to food shortages and skyrocketing food costs? Absolutely.

A global war will devastate supply chains. What will happen to global food supplies? What will happen when stores can no longer stock their shelves? Think about where you live. If the grocery store shelves are empty, how long before most of your neighbors run out of food? It's likely the world will face such conditions following the global war in Revelation 6. "War and slaughter everywhere" will wreak havoc on global distribution.

When supply chains break, the basic laws of supply and demand will kick in. Prices for food and other life necessities will skyrocket. Although the disruption will not be permanent, it will mean much higher food prices and/or food shortages until war ends and distribution problems are fixed. Does this explain the scenario described in **Revelation 6:5**? It's possible.

Once nanofactories appear, a world economic crisis will ensue. Every sector of the economy will be transformed in some way. The change will be rapid and demonstrable. Many companies will be ruined, unable to compete against an endless supply of cheap generic products. Many people who once had a high standard of living will find themselves in poverty.

Government to the Rescue

If the war and famine outlined in Revelation 6 comes from the introduction of nanofactories, then nanofactories will also offer the solution. As said before, nanofactories will lead to an abundance of food, clean drinking water, and everyday consumer products. However, it will take some time for these benefits to reach everyone in the world. Especially in the aftermath of a global war. Think about the impact hurricanes and other natural disasters have on everyday life. It takes a while for things to return to normal. Nanofactories will have a similar impact on the entire global economy, especially when introduced in tandem with a global war. Until a new normal settles in, many will experience scarcity rather than abundance. Who will they turn to? God? I wish. Unfortunately, most people will turn to the same place they usually turn in an emergency – government.

Already, we hear talk of "universal basic income" in response to the coming economic changes. This means the government will pay everyone a basic income whether they work or not. Champions of this idea say it will liberate people from work. People could then channel their creative energies into "higher" pursuits. Critics say it will kill initiative and result in widespread dependence on government. Depending on the individual, it will probably do both. Either way, as more and more jobs become automated, you'll hear further calls for universal basic income.

The Antichrist will likely roll out something similar to this idea. With a monopoly on nanofactories and other advanced technologies, he could create the largest welfare state in human history. And unlike today, such a system will be feasible. If this happens, it explains why people will willingly give the Antichrist power over their lives. But alone it doesn't explain how he obtains such vast power over every economic transaction. The Bible says no one will be able to buy or sell without his permission (***Revelation 13:17***). Does this mean everyone will be on government welfare? No. But the arrival of nanofactories does offer a possible explanation for how this happens.

Why? Because a world of war and famine isn't all nanofactories will bring. They'll also transform the global monetary system.

The Coming Cashless Society

The Bible says a time will come when a global dictator requires everyone on earth to receive a mark on the right hand or the forehead (***Revelation 13:16***). Those without the mark won't be able to buy or sell *anything* (***Revelation 13:17***). For centuries, Christians have wondered how this will be possible. But in recent years, the rise of advanced technology has given us a glimpse as to how it might occur.

New technologies have driven endless speculation about what the mark will be. Some think it will be an implantable microchip. Others think it will be a visible tattoo. Still others think it will involve bar codes, social security numbers, or RFID chips. And on and on. The fact is, we don't know. And it won't be known until the mark actually appears.

However, we can know this – the technology is here to make such a mark possible. To control every buy and sell transaction in the world, the Antichrist will need to set up a system capable of tracking every transaction. And thanks to modern technology, we can easily envision such a system. Much of the foundation is in place. Electronic payments are already a way of life, and they foreshadow the coming of a cashless society. But you know what? A cashless society is not only possible – it's inevitable. Nanofactories **guarantee** it.

How can I be so certain? Because nanofactories will transform another industry – the business of printing money. Once nanofactories appear, cash and coins will become worthless. They'll be relics of the past. Items more fit for a museum than your wallet. Why do I say this? Because nanofactories will put immense power in the hands of everyone on earth. And they'll be a dream come true for counterfeiters.

In a world of new technologies where *every molecule* can be perfectly positioned, it won't be possible to stop counterfeiters. They'll be able to create exact replicas of every national currency. And when that happens, the world will be flooded with fake money – worthless fake money. And since no one will be able to tell the difference between the fake cash and the real cash, **both** will be worthless.

Counterfeiting will be impossible to stop. You can use all the special paper you want. You can add security strips, watermarks, raised printing, and color-shifting ink. You can add hundreds of new features. It doesn't matter. Desktop devices able to create exact replicas of any nation's currency will be everywhere. Short of embedding currency with smart-chips linked to a government-controlled verification system, there is *no* way to avoid widespread counterfeiting in a world of nanofactories. And if you need to put electronic verification devices in cash, why bother making it at all? Why not just make all transactions electronic?

In essence, that's what we see now. The majority of buy and sell transactions are electronic. Debit cards, credit cards, and bank transfer services such as PayPal are the most common forms of payment. It's rare to see anyone pay cash anymore. Think about your daily routine. Whether it's the coffee shop, the grocery store, or Walmart, how do the people around you pay for what they're buying? If you take the time to look, I bet you'll see a lot of credit and debit cards – maybe even a mobile phone payment. How many people use cash? And of those, how many are under the age of 40? Hardly any, right? In fact, many people under the age of 30 don't even know how to write a check. The younger you are, the less likely you are to use *any* cash. Cash is already becoming obsolete. We're on the verge of a cashless society right now.

So why does any of this matter? This is why. At some point in the near future, the Antichrist will seize power. When he does, a global electronic payment system will already exist. While it remains to be seen how he will control *every* buy and sell transaction, the stage is being set. Convenience has already led to most transactions going electronic. And soon, new technologies will make all paper currency obsolete. This will eventually create a situation where a global government *could* monitor and control every economic transaction on earth. Such a system has never existed in the nearly 2,000 years since the Book of Revelation said the Antichrist would control all buy and sell transactions (***Revelation 13:17***). In fact, such a system was impossible for all of those nearly 2,000 years. But today? Today is different. We see the groundwork for such a system coming into place.

Conclusion

Faced with the global economic conditions described in the Book of Revelation, many people will willingly support the Antichrist. The story of Joseph in the Book of Genesis foreshadows this future event. But hunger isn't the only reason the world will follow him. Remember, the post-Tower of Babel conditions currently dividing the world will disappear. Language barriers will disappear. National borders will go away. The world will be united, and after the initial chaos, resources will become abundant.

People will support the Antichrist not only out of necessity, but out of a willing desire to do so. In fact, the Bible tells us much of the world will worship the Antichrist **because** of his power (***Revelation 13:4***), just as people worshipped Caesar two thousand years ago.

Just as the people willingly gave their wealth and power to Pharaoh in exchange for grain, the future world will willingly cede its power to the Antichrist. Like Pharaoh, he'll consolidate power – only his power won't be confined to Egypt. He'll have absolute authority over the whole world. He'll control every nation, race, and people (***Revelation 13:7***). And he'll gain this power the same way Pharaoh gained his. People will give it to him. And they won't just give it to him because of fear, hunger, or a need to survive. They'll give it to him because they'll believe he's the Messiah.

CHAPTER 10

Are You The Messiah?

WHILE JOHN THE Baptist was in prison, his disciples came and told him about Jesus, His miracles, and what He was saying and doing. So John sent them to find Jesus and ask Him this, "Are you the Messiah? Are you the one we've been expecting?"

What Jesus said leaves no doubt as to His identity. Jesus told them, "Go. Tell John this. The blind see. The deaf hear. The lame walk. The lepers are healed. The dead are raised to life, and the Good News is preached to the poor" (***Luke 7:18-22, Matthew 11:2-6***). This satisfied John. Why? Because John's disciples *saw* and *heard* these miracles (***Luke 7:22***). They didn't just take Jesus' word for it (although they could have). They were eyewitnesses.

John knew the Messianic prophecies. So when he heard about these miracles, he knew who Jesus was. He knew they signaled the Messiah's arrival. He knew hundreds of years before Jesus walked the earth, Isaiah said when the Messiah comes, He will open the eyes of the blind and unplug the ears of the deaf. He knew Isaiah said the lame will leap like a deer and the mute will sing with joy (***Isaiah 35:5-6***). So in John's mind, this settled the question. Jesus was the Messiah.

But what about everyone else?

Many other people witnessed the miracles of Jesus firsthand. After meeting with Jesus, it was common to see the following… The mute could speak. The deaf could hear. The paralyzed could walk. And the blind could see. Because of these miracles, many believed in Jesus. But others **refused** to believe, even though these miracles verified His identity as the Son of God. What did Jesus

Chapter 10

say about these people? He said, "I have come in my Father's name, and you refused to receive me. But a day will come when another man comes in his own name, and him you will receive" (*John 5:43-44*).

Go ahead and read that again. It says when "another man comes in his own name," the world will receive him. Think this is just an offhand remark? I don't think so. You should know Jesus well enough to know He doesn't make *any* offhand remarks. This is a prophecy of a specific future event. Jesus is saying, while the world rejected Him as the true Messiah, it will one day embrace a false Messiah – the Antichrist.

RISE OF THE ANTICHRIST

Imagine if Satan came to earth and used promises of world peace and miracle healings to trick the world into following a false messiah? Do you think this would be effective? After all, Jesus performed true miracles and many of the people who saw them still refused to believe in Him. Wouldn't those same skeptics also deny someone else? Even in the face of supposed "miracles"? According to Jesus, they won't.

In the days before Jesus returns, the Bible says the world will be a place of deception, counterfeit miracles, and false prophets. These evils will deceive an untold number of people throughout the world. In fact, Jesus Himself said the signs and wonders of these false messiahs and false prophets will be so amazing they will (if it were possible) deceive God's chosen people (*Matthew 24:24*).

Did you catch that? Jesus didn't simply say false messiahs and false prophets will appear in the end times. Such people have appeared in every generation. What Jesus said is *these* false prophets and false messiahs are different. How? Their signs and wonders. These won't be everyday signs and wonders. The counterfeit miracles of these false prophets will be so extraordinary, they'll trick even God's chosen ones (were that possible).

THE MIRACLES OF THE MESSIAH

Isaiah 35:5-6 says the Messiah will heal the blind, lame, deaf, and mute. Jesus did all these things. But He also performed other miracles. For instance, Jesus:

- Walked on water (*Matthew 14:35*)

- Fed five thousand people with two fish and five loaves of bread (***Matthew 14:15-21***)

- Turned water into wine (***John 2:1-11***)

- Raised people from the dead (***John 11:1-46, Luke 7:11-18, Matthew 9:18-26***)

- Cured fever (***Mark 1:30-31***)

- Healed lepers (***Mark 1:40-45, Luke 17:11-19***)

- Restored body parts (***Matthew 12:10-13, Luke 22:50-51***)

These are amazing feats, and they testify to the divine authority of Jesus. They validate His claim to be the Messiah. As one man asked, "When the Messiah comes, will He do greater things than this?" (***John 7:31***).

The answer is clear. Of course not. No one could be expected to do greater things than what Jesus did. Yet Jesus Himself ***did*** do greater things. He did much greater things. For example, He said, "No one can take my life from me. I lay down my life when I want, and I have the authority to pick it back up again" (***John 10:18***). Jesus backed this up when He was crucified, buried, and resurrected. This fulfilled a one-thousand-year-old Messianic prophecy from King David. It said the Messiah will not rot in the grave. Instead, He will live forever (***Psalm 16:10-11***).

Yet, despite the fulfillment of so many Messianic prophecies, several remain unfulfilled. Not because Jesus ***isn't*** the Messiah. But because Jesus is coming again.

For example, Isaiah looked forward to a time when the Messiah would personally rule over the nations of the world, settling disputes and ending all war forever. He said the nations of the world will reshape their swords into plowshares and their spears into pruning hooks, and no one will train for war anymore (***Isaiah 2:4***). Clearly, Jesus did not fulfill this prophecy two thousand years ago. But, ***He will***.

One day soon, Jesus will return to establish everlasting peace on earth. Until that day comes, the world is ripe for deception. Satan could use some of the same signs and miracles that led people to put their faith in Jesus to lead the whole world astray.

Chapter 10

THE ANTICHRIST'S COUNTERFEIT MIRACLES

In the end times, most of the world will reject Jesus as the Messiah. But, as Jesus said, they will gladly follow someone else who comes in his own name. That man is the Antichrist, and he will deceive most of the world into following him.

But how?

One way he could do this is to perform many of the same miracles Jesus performed. Keep in mind these won't be true miracles. They'll be false or counterfeit miracles. But the world won't know the difference.

We've already discussed advanced technology and its immense power. So it shouldn't surprise you to learn advanced technology will be able to perform many of the same miracles as Jesus.

Advanced technology will pave the way for machines able to repair, rebuild, and restore almost every aspect of the human body. Such machines will regenerate human cells, tissues, organs, and entire biological systems. And with them, the Antichrist can counterfeit nearly every healing miracle Jesus performed.

For example, advanced technology will eventually allow us to:

1) Restore the vocal abilities of the mute.

2) Reverse paralysis for those with spinal cord injuries.

3) Restore sight for the blind.

4) Restore all sound and hearing for the deaf.

and

5) Cure any physical disease now afflicting humans.

The end result? An era in which "the blind will see, the deaf will hear, the lame will walk, the mute will speak, and the sick will be healed."

But that's not all advanced technology will do. Advanced technology will also replicate other miracles of Jesus. Here are just a few:

Feeding the Five Thousand - Did you know the dirt outside your door most likely contains every element necessary to create a loaf of bread or a piece of fish? With the blueprint for a piece of fish or a loaf of bread, nanofactories could rearrange the basic structure of those elements and do just that. You could literally create a fish or a loaf of bread from nothing but dirt. And with enough dirt, you could feed five thousand people. In fact, with enough dirt and the right technology, you could feed the whole world.

Walking on Water - While no human can actually walk on water, advanced technology could create the illusion of walking on water. Imagine hovering platforms that move a step or two ahead of a human, just above the surface of the water. Such technology would create the same effect as walking on solid ground. But when used above water, a man will visually appear as if he's walking on water.

Turning Water into Wine - With advanced technology, you'll even be able to turn water into wine. Remember, both water and wine are products of naturally occurring chemical processes. Once we develop computers capable of directing the formation of chemical bonds, we'll be able to control those chemical processes. Assuming you have all the elements necessary to form the chemical compounds found in wine, advanced technology will open the door for turning water into wine.

Additional "Miracles"

Remember, the Antichrist's "miracles" will be counterfeit. This isn't unheard of. When Moses first approached Pharaoh, the Egyptian monarch demanded a miracle. So Moses threw down his staff, and it became a serpent. But when Pharaoh called on his own magicians, they did the same thing (***Exodus 7:11***).

The kingdom of the Antichrist will be similar. The Antichrist will be able to create counterfeit replicas of many of God's miracles. That doesn't mean he'll be just as powerful. But in the eyes of the world, he'll perform miracles Jesus never did. Here are just a few:

Fire from Heaven - The Book of Revelation says the false prophet will make fire flash down from the sky (***Revelation 13:13***). While Elijah performed this miracle (***1 Kings 18:38***), Jesus never did. Using nanofactories and other advanced technologies, human beings will gain complete mastery over the material universe. In such a world, if the false prophet called down fire from the sky, he could make it happen.

Everlasting Life - With its ability to repair and regenerate human cells, tissues, and organs, advanced technology will promise dramatic improvements in human health. The Antichrist will promise perpetual youth and good health as well as an escape from death.

But again, this power will only extend to the physical world. True life comes from God. Your soul belongs to Christ. It doesn't matter if you acknowledge His power or not (*John 5:25-30*). But that truth will be hidden from the people who belong to this world, and they will believe the lie, thinking advanced technology can make them immortal.

Peace on Earth - As discussed in Chapter 7, advanced technology will lead to global government. With a single unified government, no competing militaries, and no language barriers, it will appear as though war is forever a part of the past.

But again, this will be a lie. Only Jesus can bring lasting peace. In the absence of the Holy Spirit, man's fallen nature makes war inevitable. Sin is the root cause of all human conflict (*James 4:1*), and no technology (no matter how advanced) can cleanse the world of sin.

Despite humanity's sinful nature, for a time, the world will appear to be at peace. The absolute power of the Antichrist's global government will make war seem impossible. Under such conditions, the world could be deceived into believing this false peace is eternal. Since the Bible says when the Messiah comes, "nation will no longer fight nation, nor will they train for war anymore" (*Isaiah 2:4*), this could lead to worship of the Antichrist (*Revelation 13:4*).

Can you begin to see how the world will be deceived?

The World's Reaction

In a day and age when people are obsessed with materialism, a man with absolute control over the physical world will appear to be God Himself. But such a man falls far short of the glory of God (*Romans 3:23*). God is the only one in absolute control. He rules the entire universe, and that includes far more than the physical world.

Jesus didn't simply heal the sick, He cast out demons (***Matthew 8:28-34, Luke 11:14, Mark 1:34, Luke 4:41***). He granted forgiveness of sins (***Luke 7:48, Matthew 9:2***). Even with the aid of advanced technology, the Antichrist will ***never*** have these powers.

But despite his shortcomings, the Antichrist will mesmerize the world. Think about it. How will the world react to a person who unites the human race in peace and prosperity? How about a man who eliminates all disease, handicaps, and poverty? Or one who promises you'll live forever?

For much of the world, the Antichrist will appear to bring about what Peter, the apostles, and most first century Jews expected the Messiah to bring – the Messianic kingdom described in the Book of Isaiah. A world of peace (***Isaiah 2:4***), health (***Isaiah 35:5-6***), everlasting life (***Psalm 16:10-11***), and material abundance (***Joel 3:18***). The Antichrist will appear to usher in this kingdom. But it will be a kingdom of lies.

The signs and wonders of the Antichrist will deceive people who believe they are supernatural acts of God. Instead, they'll be satanic in origin. In a letter to Timothy, Paul revealed why people will be deceived. He said a time is coming when people will follow their own desires. They'll look for teachers who will tell them whatever their itching ears want to hear (***2 Timothy 4:3-4***).

Simply put, people will be fooled in the last days because they'll ***want*** to be fooled. While this sounds foolish (and it is), it's true. People will believe in the signs and wonders of the Antichrist because they'll want to believe the lies and false promises that go with them.

It's easy to see how a Christ-rejecting world will fall prey to these deceptions. With the aid of advanced technology, the Antichrist could copy many of the miracles Jesus performed. The lame will walk. The deaf will hear. The mute will speak. The blind will see. War will end, and material abundance will be everywhere.

According to ***Isaiah 35:4-6***, these are the very same things that will happen "when your God comes." The Antichrist will tell the world he is their Savior. It's a lie. But it's not the only lie he'll tell. He'll spread another lie, and the world's "itching ears" will readily embrace it.

CHAPTER 11

The Great Lie

IN THE 16ᵀᴴ Century, Spanish conquistador Juan Ponce de Leon traversed the New World in search of the Fountain of Youth, a mystical source of water able to restore the youth of anyone who drank it or bathed in it. The legend tells us Ponce de Leon and his band of explorers searched every river, brook, spring, or puddle they could find. But of course, they never found the Fountain of Youth. It was nothing but a myth. In fact, many historians believe Ponce de Leon's search for the Fountain of Youth was itself a myth.

Either way, the legend of such a fountain goes back to the earliest days of humanity. The Greek historian Herodotus mentioned such a fountain. So do writings dating back to the Roman Empire. The Crusaders also talked about the fountain. My point? Throughout history, mankind has held a deep-seated desire to reverse the aging process. A way to defeat death and live on forever. And while you and I may laugh at the idea of a Fountain of Youth, you know what? It's a legend people still pursue to this day.

THE QUEST FOR IMMORTALITY

Whether it's anti-aging creams or plastic surgery, people of our day and time want to reverse the aging process too. We may not be in search of an actual fountain to provide eternal youth. But we still dream of it. And think about this for a moment. What if it's possible?

That's right. What if it's possible to stay young and live forever? Quite a few people believe it is. And they believe humans are on the verge of making it happen. Think it's impossible? Maybe.

Chapter 11

But imagine your body is like a car. It shouldn't be too hard. After all, a car is a machine. It has moving parts with defined functions. Likewise, your body is also a machine. Granted, it's a biological machine. But it's a machine nonetheless. Just like a car, it has moving parts with defined functions. And just like your car does what you tell it to do, your body does what your brain tells it to do.

Now, what do you do when your car wears out? You get a new one, right? What if you could do the same thing with your body? What if you could get a new body when the old one wears out? What if you could replace parts as they age? Or regenerate tissue on a regular basis?

In the same way, imagine your brain is like your computer. But instead of the files and data you keep on your computer, the files and data in your brain are all the memories and knowledge of a lifetime. What do you do when your old computer becomes broken or obsolete? You simply get a new one, right? And when you do, what happens to all the files on the old computer? You transfer them from the old one (or a backup) onto the new one. What if you could do the same thing with your brain? What if you could backup all the information in your brain? Then, if something happened to you, what if you could upload that information into a new brain in a new body?

If you could do this, you could (in theory) live forever. This ability to liberate ourselves from our physical bodies is a fairly accurate description of the transhumanist vision of the future.

It makes sense some people will aspire to this. After all, our bodies get old. They decay and eventually stop working. And when they do, a person has no backup. When they die, a lifetime of memories and knowledge are lost forever. To many, this is unacceptable.

To those people, death is an enemy. And many of them believe they can make death itself obsolete. They believe they can stop the process of aging and conquer death forever. How? In the same way just described. By uploading their unique thoughts and brain patterns into a "more reliable vessel," one better equipped for the long-term than a frail human body. Once that's done, backup copies of their brain can be stored on a decentralized network such as the Internet. In this way, many people believe they can "live forever." As we approach the singularity, advanced technologies will make this transhumanist vision of the future our new reality.

As humans unlock the mysteries of the physical universe, many will choose to merge with advanced technology. They'll build a direct connection between their brains and the Internet. They'll implant all the capabilities of modern day smartphones into their bodies. They'll replace their flesh and blood bodies with new metallic ones. Or they'll put on indestructible bodysuits that make Ironman look like a weakling. And I'm sure they'll incorporate new technologies we have yet to imagine.

By merging with technology, people will believe they can achieve immortality. No more fatal diseases or car crashes. But while these technologies will be powerful, and the people using them will be powerful, advanced technology will *never* overcome death. How can I be so sure?

Because advanced technology doesn't address the root problem of death - *sin*. That's right. Despite all our advances and all our breakthroughs, human beings have yet to solve the problem of human evil. It's the one disease we can't cure with medical breakthroughs. We're born into sin, and our sin passes from generation to generation. And ultimately, sin is what leads to death (***Romans 6:23***).

Only one thing can conquer death. Only one thing can blot out our sin. It's the blood of Jesus Christ (***Ephesians 1:7***). No technological breakthrough can take the place of His blood. No invention of man can save our souls, and no advancement will sidestep the Day of Judgment (***Romans 2:5-6***).

Nevertheless, people will tell themselves otherwise. Pride will lead them to buy into the idea they can cheat death. They'll chase after such lies and myths. But why? It's simple. They'll buy into these lies because they'll *want* to believe them.

Remember, Paul said a time is coming when people will ignore sound teaching. Instead, they'll follow their own desires and seek out teachers who will tell them what their "itching ears" want to hear (***2 Timothy 4:3-4***). In other words, people will ignore the truth. In its place, they'll look for people who will tell them what they want to hear.

Such teachers won't be hard to find in the end times. Many people will be willing to tell the world what it wants to hear. But one such teacher will stand tall among all the rest. He'll tickle the world's itching ears, and the world will follow him down a path to destruction.

Chapter 11

FOLLOWING THE FALSE MESSIAH

Remember what John the Baptist asked Jesus? He asked Jesus, "Are you the Messiah?" Jesus said, "Go. Tell John this. The blind see. The deaf hear. The lame walk. The lepers are healed. The dead are raised to life, and the Good News is preached to the poor" (**Luke 7:18-22, Matthew 11:2-6**).

In John's mind this proved Jesus was the Messiah. Why? Again, John knew the Messianic prophecies. He knew Isaiah said the Messiah will open the eyes of the blind and unplug the ears of the deaf (**Isaiah 35:5**). He knew Isaiah said the lame will leap like a deer and the mute will sing with joy (**Isaiah 35:6**). So in John's mind, this settled the question. Jesus was the Messiah.

We've already addressed how advanced technology could bring about these same things. What if the Antichrist uses this same passage from Isaiah to claim *he's* the Messiah? The Book of Revelation tells us he'll use false miracles to deceive the people of this world (**Revelation 13:13**). What if he goes even further? What if he tells the world he can conquer death? What if people believe the transhumanist promise they can live forever? What if the Antichrist uses scripture to proclaim himself the Messiah?

After all, the Bible says, *"When our perishable earthly bodies have been transformed into heavenly bodies that will never die - then at last the Scripture will come true: 'Death is swallowed up in victory. O death, where is your victory? O death, where is your sting?'"* **1 Corinthians 15:54-55** (NLT)

What if the Antichrist uses advanced technology to claim he's fulfilled this prophecy? What if he says his arrival is no accident – that death has been swallowed up in victory because *he* is the Messiah? Will the people of the world believe him? Remember, Jesus said one day the whole world will follow a false messiah (**John 5:43**). Imagine if the person they follow says they can live forever? What if he says they can go on sinning and avoid death forever? Would that "tickle their itching ears" (**2 Timothy 4:3-4**)?

Like every false messiah before him, the Antichrist will convince his followers he's the answer to the world's problems. Paul tells us those who become caught in this man's web of deceit will be guilty because they freely choose to enjoy evil while denying the truth (**2 Thessalonians 2:10**).

If this man arrives at the same time as the singularity, it's quite possible he could use the bold promises of transhumanism to convince the world he is the long-awaited Messiah. By taking bible prophecy out of context, the Antichrist could deceive untold numbers of people. And in their pride, the people of this world will willingly follow him. The Bible says they'll buy into "a great lie" he tells them. As Paul says, God will send the world a strong delusion so they believe "the lie" of the Antichrist (***2 Thessalonians 2:11***).

So what is this "great lie"? It's the first recorded lie in human history. To find the answer, we need to refer to yet another well-known Sunday school story. It's a story about a man, a woman, and a serpent's enticing lie.

The Great Lie

When God created Adam and Eve, he gave them free reign over a beautiful land known as the Garden of Eden. In Eden, Adam and Eve had fellowship with God. The Creator of the Universe provided them with food, water, fellowship, purpose, and everything they needed to live a life of abundance.

God only placed one restriction on Adam and Eve. "You can freely eat of every tree in the garden," He said. "Every tree except the tree of the knowledge of good and evil" (***Genesis 2:16-17***). Adam and Eve lived well in the Garden of Eden until the day serpent arrived.

One day, the serpent asked Eve, "Did God really say you must not eat the fruit from that tree?"

"Only the fruit from the tree in the middle of the garden," she said. "God said you must not eat it or you will die."

"You won't die," the serpent replied. "God knows if you eat it your eyes will be opened, and you will be like God, knowing both good and evil." Eve believed the serpent, and she and Adam ate of the fruit (***Genesis 3:1-6***).

From the very beginning, the serpent undermined God's Word. He planted a seed of doubt with these words, "Did God *really* say..." He then told the first recorded lie in human history. "You won't die," he said. "God knows if you eat it your eyes will be opened, and you will be like God, knowing both good and evil" (***Genesis 3:4-5***).

Not only is this the first lie, it's ***the great lie***. It's the natural offspring of the original sin – pride. It's the same lie Satan believed when he rebelled against God (***Isaiah 14:12-15***). And it's the same lie the world will believe when it rebels in the end times.

The Antichrist will tell it to a world eager to hear it. So what is this great lie?

"You will be like God."
This is the great lie.

THE PINNACLE OF PRIDE

In the end times, humans will tell themselves, "You will be like God." It's an idea built on a lie. What greater lie can be told than this – mankind can enjoy heavenly bodies and immortality without first shedding their sinful nature? It's a lie leading straight to destruction.

While Jesus said, "You will be like gods" (***John 10:34***), He did not mean humans could achieve "god status" apart from the God of Abraham, Isaac, and Jacob. In fact, He said, "I am the vine. If you are cut off from me, you will wither" (***John 15:6***). No. To say, "I will be like God" apart from Jesus is to challenge God's authority. It's the pinnacle of human pride and arrogance.

Make no mistake. God detests pride (***Proverbs 16:5***). It leads to disgrace (***Proverbs 11:2***) and destruction (***Proverbs 16:18***). Life never ends well for those filled with pride. God promises to punish them and tear down everything that is exalted (***Isaiah 2:12***).

Only a heart filled with pride could look in the mirror and say, "You will be like God." But in their arrogance, this is exactly what the people of this world will do. They will believe they can become like God – not by becoming His adopted sons and daughters (***Ephesians 1:5***), but by placing themselves on God's throne. And just as God hardened the heart of Pharaoh (***Exodus 9:12***), He will do the same to the end time inhabitants of the earth. God will cause them to become so deluded, they believe the lie (***2 Thessalonians 2:11***).

The same lie which brought sin into the world will be the same lie which sparks the ultimate rebellion against God Almighty. Humans will come full circle. Modern day Tower of Babel architects will resume their efforts to build a "monument to human greatness." The exponential growth of advanced technology will give humans unprecedented control over the physical world. Control so powerful "***nothing will be impossible for them***."

In their arrogance, people will believe they are:

1) Immortal

2) All-Knowing

and…

3) "Just like God"

When this happens, humanity's desire will be the same as Satan's desire. Centuries ago, Isaiah revealed Satan's deepest desire:

"How you are fallen from heaven, O shining star, son of the morning! You have been thrown down to the earth, you who destroyed the nations of the world. For you said to yourself, 'I will ascend to heaven and set my throne above God's stars. I will preside on the mountain of the gods far away in the north. I will climb to the highest heavens and be like the Most High.'"
Isaiah 14:12-14 (NLT)

Satan's burning desire is to "be like the Most High." His number one goal is to be "just like God."

As we approach Armageddon, this won't be Satan's desire alone. It will be all of mankind's desire. The world will freely join Satan in his rebellious attempt to seize the throne of God. Because without Jesus Christ, fallen mankind's ambition is the same as Lucifer's.

Think I'm crazy? Think it's unreasonable to believe people will one day view themselves as all-powerful gods? Think again. History tells us otherwise. We've seen it time and time again. We've seen it all through history. And we see it today. We see it in New Age writers and gurus who tell their followers "power is within you" and "you shape your own destiny." We see it in counselors and personal development coaches who say the same thing. And we've seen it in the kings and emperors of the past who viewed themselves as gods.

The Antichrist will see himself this way. He'll think of himself as immortal, all-knowing, all-powerful, and ever-present. In short, he'll see himself as God. As such, he'll demand worship (**2 Thessalonians 2:4**, **Revelation 13:8**) and seek to fulfill Satan's original desire (**Isaiah 14**).

But have no doubt. He will fail. And he will fail miserably.

Chapter 11

NOTHING BUT EMPTY PROMISES

The Antichrist will fail. The Bible foretells it (***Revelation 19:20***). Transhumanism will also fail. How can I be so sure? Because the empty promises of transhumanism are nothing new:

- Human immortality
- The end of suffering
- The end of starvation
- The end of disease
- The end of disabilities

These are lofty goals. Throughout history, almost every person on earth has yearned for them. And some will ultimately achieve these goals. But they will ***not*** achieve these goals through advanced technology.

Remember, humans are infected with sin. And sin is the root cause of death, suffering, disease, and all the ills of this world. In short, sin is the root cause of almost everything transhumanism promises to solve. And since transhumanism and advanced technology do nothing to address sin, they'll fail.

If this is the case, why do I insist ***some*** people will overcome these ills? Because some people have placed their faith in something far more powerful than advanced technology. Something far more powerful than human ingenuity. Something far more powerful than the promises of transhumanism.

What is this great power?

It's the blood of Jesus Christ.

And because of their faith in Jesus, these people ***will*** witness:

1) The end of starvation and disease...
"On each side of the river grew a tree of life, bearing twelve crops of fruit, with a fresh crop each month. The leaves were used for medicine to heal the nations." **Revelation 22:2** (NLT)

2) The end of disabilities...
"And when He comes, He will open the eyes of the blind and unplug the ears

of the deaf. The lame will leap like a deer, and those who cannot speak will sing for joy!" **Isaiah 35:5-6** (NLT)

And

3) The end of death and suffering...
"There will be no more death or sorrow or crying or pain. All these things are gone forever." **Revelation 21:4** (NLT)

All of these hopes will be realized when Jesus returns to earth and sets up His everlasting kingdom.

The problem with transhumanism is it seeks to achieve these goals through human power. It's an attempt to sidestep the redemptive blood of Jesus as shed on the cross. And because of that, transhumanism is a dead end. It can't deliver on its promises.

Jesus is the only way to heaven (*1 Timothy 2:5-6*). Every other path is a dead end. Those who try to get to heaven any other way are like thieves and robbers trying to climb over a wall.

Jesus said, "I am the gate" (*John 10:9*). He is the only path to heaven. Jesus said the only way to achieve salvation is through Him. No one can conquer death through any other means than through Jesus (*John 14:6*). This is why the transhumanist vision of heaven on earth will ultimately fail.

Nevertheless, many will strive in vain to achieve the empty promises of the transhumanist vision. They'll reject Jesus. They'll reject wisdom. And they'll chase after a lie.

What makes this so sad is everything they seek is readily available right now. An end to suffering. World peace. Victory over death. All these things are available free of charge.

All of them can be realized through faith in Jesus. In fact, they can *only* be realized through faith in Jesus. Unfortunately, the world of today rejects this idea. They see it as foolish (*1 Corinthians 1:18*). The world in the end times will also see it as foolish. Pride will lead the last generation to reject Jesus in favor of their own power.

Chapter 11

THE COMING CONFLICT

As the end times generation lives out its Garden of Eden fantasy of "being like God," they will place themselves in direct opposition to the Lord of the Universe. This is nothing new. What is new is the world will no longer be satisfied with simply breaking God's laws and defaming His name.

As the Tribulation comes to a close, humanity will declare its independence. Humans will reject God, and like Satan, they'll seek to "ascend above the heights" and "be like the Most High" (***Isaiah 14:14***).

The Bible says human beings will attempt to usurp the authority of God and dethrone the Lord Almighty. The age-old rebellion against God will spill over from the spiritual realm into the physical realm. Humanity will declare war on the God of Abraham, Isaac, and Jacob. They'll set out to conquer Him and remove Him from the throne of heaven. Think I'm nuts? Think again. Because that's exactly what the Bible says.

CHAPTER 12

The War to End All Wars (Man vs. God)

APPROXIMATELY 200 YEARS before Jesus, a Greek king named Antiochus Epiphanes outlawed Jewish worship. He attacked the Temple in Jerusalem, stole its treasures, and sacrificed pigs on the altar. He even placed a statue of Zeus in the Temple and demanded its worship. His evil decrees sparked the Maccabean revolt and eventually led to the liberation of Jerusalem and the events which are the basis for the annual Hanukkah celebration.

Antiochus Epiphanes personified evil. He thought of himself as a god, and he demanded worship. In fact, the very name "Epiphanes" (which he gave himself) means "Illustrious One" or "God Manifest." He obviously thought highly of himself. But you know what? He wasn't alone.

Many throughout history did the same thing. Nebuchadnezzar thought of himself as a god, and he demanded worship (***Daniel 3:4-6***). The Pharaohs demanded worship. The Roman emperors demanded worship. Even in modern times, the leader of North Korea demands worship.

Does this surprise you? I doubt it. It shouldn't surprise anyone. The human heart is sick. It's filled with wickedness, envy, slander, and evil thoughts of every kind (***Mark 7:21-22***). Worst of all, it's filled with pride. It's in a state of constant rebellion against God.

Will the human heart be any different in the end times? No. The Antichrist will also demand worship (***2 Thessalonians 2:4***). Like Pharaoh, he will challenge the Great I AM (***Exodus 5:2***). Unfortunately, the Bible says most of the world will follow him.

Chapter 12

Man's Ultimate Goal

Like the world of today, the world of the end times will be a world awash with information, but starving for wisdom. Human technology will increase exponentially from now until the very day Jesus returns. But no matter how powerful our technology becomes, it can never overcome human imperfection. Technology cannot rid us of our rebellious nature. In fact, it's just the opposite. Instead of taming our sinful nature, technology will ***amplify*** it.

Eventually, rapidly advancing technology and human nature will converge at Armageddon. But not the Armageddon most people think. Remember, Armageddon has nothing to do with mushroom clouds, comets, or asteroids. It's a battle between two armies. It's the climactic battle in a longstanding war. And it's NOT a human vs. human conflict.

Remember, the Book of Revelation says no one will be able to make war against the Antichrist (***Revelation 13:4***). He rules a ***global*** empire (***Revelation 13:7***). He controls every detail of human life, including who can buy and who can sell (***Revelation 13:17***). If that's the case, what nation or nations will fight against him at Armageddon?

You know the answer. No nation will oppose the Antichrist at Armageddon. The truth is much worse. Instead of fighting against the Antichrist, the nations of the world will ***join*** him. That's right. Almost all of humanity will gather at Armageddon to fight ***alongside*** the Antichrist, not against him. If that's true, who will they fight against? You already know the answer to that question too. The real question is whether or not you're willing to accept it.

The Bible says the Antichrist and his followers gather at Armageddon for one purpose – to fight God.

That's right. The armies at Armageddon don't gather to fight each other. They gather to fight the God of the Universe. These humans will view themselves as gods. They'll seek lofty goals. They'll set out to conquer death, disease, poverty, and war. They'll also set out to conquer the physical, spiritual, and moral constraints of God. Because He's the very one they gather against at Armageddon.

Why will the end times generation attack God? The Book of Revelation provides us with a clue. In it, God pours out His wrath on a rebellious world (***Revelation 6:17***). In the Tribulation, God's judgments include – but aren't limited to – global war (***Revelation 6:4***), global famine (***Revelation 6:6***), widespread death (***Revelation 6:8***), stars falling to the earth (***Revelation 6:13***), a rain of hail and fire mixed with blood (***Revelation 8:7***), a five-month global plague of locusts (***Revelation 9:3-5***), death of one-third of the earth's people (***Revelation 9:15***), no rain for three and a half years (***Revelation 11:6***), rivers and oceans turned to blood (***Revelation 11:6***), a global plague of sores (***Revelation 16:2***), the death of everything in the sea (***Revelation 16:3***), the transformation of all rivers and springs to blood (***Revelation 16:4***), scorching fire from the sun (***Revelation 16:8***), global darkness (***Revelation 16:10***), a global earthquake so great islands disappear and mountains are leveled (***Revelation 16:20***), and a terrible hailstorm with 75-pound hailstones (***Revelation 16:21***). Does this sound terrible? It will be. All this pain and suffering will strike the world in a seven year period, and the end times generation will blame God for all of it.

How can I be so sure? Because the Bible says so. It says the people of the earth acknowledge the judgments come from God (***Revelation 6:15-17; 18:10***). So what do they do in response?

They curse Him for it.

That's right. They curse God. They curse Him because He has control over all the plagues (***Revelation 16:9***). They curse Him because of their pains and sores (***Revelation 16:11***), and they curse Him because of the terrible hailstorm (***Revelation 16:21***). The Bible also says the people of the earth give each other presents to celebrate the death of God's two prophets "who had tormented them" (***Revelation 11:10***). That's right. The end times generation will openly revile God. They'll hate Him.

And while it's sad to say, most of the world's inhabitants will harden their hearts in the face of God's judgment. Unlike the people of Nineveh (***Jonah 3:5-10***), they won't repent and turn to God (***Revelation 9:20; 16:11***). Instead, they'll set out to destroy Him.

Think that's ridiculous? I understand why you might think so. But as humans become more and more powerful, isn't it bound to happen? As their power grows, the end times generation will seek to control every atom of the earth, solar system, and universe. They'll set out to infuse the universe with their idea of "order" and "intelligence." This ambition can only lead to one place – a direct conflict with God. And that conflict is Armageddon.

Chapter 12

Breaking "God's Chains"

Need an example? Just look at Psalm 2. It says the nations of the world will plot against God. They'll gather together to take on the Lord and his anointed one, Jesus (***Psalm 2:1-2***).

But why? What's their motive? Why would mankind try to wage an actual physical war against God? Again, Psalm 2 gives us the answer.

It says humans will attempt to "break the chains and shackles that enslave them" (***Psalm 2:3***). In other words, the human race will see itself as held in bondage. They'll see the God of Abraham, Isaac, and Jacob as an evil task master. They'll see Him as a ruler they need to liberate themselves from. Because of this, they'll try to break free from the physical, spiritual, and moral constraints God placed on the human race.

Of course, this is complete nonsense. God hasn't enslaved the world. What holds mankind in bondage is ***sin***, not the physical, spiritual, or moral constraints of God. But the world won't see it that way. They'll think God is the problem. They'll willingly believe the great lie, "You will be like God." And they'll willingly follow a man the Bible calls "the son of perdition" (***2 Thessalonians 2:3***).

The War to End All Wars

At this point, you might be thinking, *"Okay, Britt. If the Battle of Armageddon is a literal physical battle between God Almighty and the people of this world, how come this is the first time I'm hearing about it? Aren't you making this up?"* No. I'm not making it up. All you have to do is read your Bible.

But if all you have to do is read your Bible, how come people haven't been talking about this for years? The answer is simple. It's not common knowledge because most Christians throughout history "spiritualized" the verses about Armageddon. In other words, they looked at what the Bible said, and then said, "It doesn't really mean what it says." They rejected a literal interpretation in favor of a symbolic one. Why did they do this? The reason is simple. Because taking the Bible literally means human beings will one day physically attack God, and this seems utterly ridiculous. After all, how could any man fight God? How can any human being attempt, much less dare to believe, they can defeat God?

Just the thought of such a thing is hard to grasp. We think it's impossible. And because we think it's impossible, we've interpreted these verses as symbolic of nothing more than a spiritual struggle against God. But as you've seen, the Bible is clear. The Antichrist and his followers challenge the King of kings in battle.

Something else is clear too. To challenge God, the Antichrist and his followers will need to be far more powerful than the humans of today. We've already discussed how transhumanism can create such humans, but is there any biblical evidence pointing to this power? Yes.

THE ULTIMATE REBELLION

After Jesus was baptized, Satan tempted Him in the desert for forty days and forty nights. During this time, Satan told Jesus if he worshipped him, he would give him all the nations of the world (***Matthew 4:8-9***).

The Antichrist will receive this same offer. But unlike Jesus, he will accept it. The Antichrist will have unrivaled global power, and no one will be able to stand against him (***Revelation 13:4***). Since the dawn of history, no human has held the type of power this man will have.

The Bible describes the Antichrist as so powerful he's able to attack "heavenly armies." He throws heavenly beings to ground and tramples them (***Daniel 8:10***).

In case you missed that, I'll say it again.

The Antichrist actually throws **heavenly beings** – angels – to the ground and tramples them. There it is in black and white. Clear, irrefutable evidence the Antichrist is not a normal human being. He's far different from the rulers and dictators who came before him. And the Bible paints a picture of a man with power well beyond all previous humans.

This immense power enables the Antichrist to cause an extraordinary amount of destruction (***Daniel 8:24***). The Bible says he's so powerful, he challenges the Commander of heaven's armies, Jesus Christ (***Daniel 8:11***). Again, let's not gloss over that statement. A mere man challenges the Lion of Judah – the very Creator of the Universe. Does this surprise you? It shouldn't. God foretold this very conflict in the Garden of Eden (***Genesis 3:15***).

Again, think about the power of the Antichrist. It's beyond anything we've ever seen from fallen man. He doesn't just rule over humans. He attacks and defeats angels (***Daniel 8:10***), and he attacks God Himself (***Daniel 8:11***).

Chapter 12

With the aid of advanced technology, he will be an invincible global dictator. No rival nations will exist to threaten his rule. He'll have a ruthlessly efficient global police state at his disposal. Who could possibly stop him? Who could possibly make war against such a man? These are the questions people will ask themselves in the end times (***Revelation 13:4***). In the eyes of the world, the answer will be, "No one."

But the world is wrong. The Bible says the Antichrist will be broken, ***but not by human power*** (***Daniel 8:23-25***).

Like the Tower of Babel generation, the arrogance of the Antichrist and those who worship him will reach all the way to heaven. He'll take on Jesus in battle, and the Antichrist will be broken. The Bible makes it clear the Antichrist will not be defeated by any human army, but by Jesus Christ Himself (***Daniel 8:23-25***). And you know what? Jesus will have no problem at all defeating the Antichrist. It won't even be close.

God's Ultimate Victory

When Jesus first came, He came as the Lamb of God (***John 1:29***). "I came not to judge the world," Jesus said, "But to save it" (***John 3:17***). When Jesus comes at Armageddon, it will be a different story. He'll come as the Lion of Judah (***Revelation 5:5***). The Bible says He'll bring punishment to the proud rulers of the earth. Destruction will fall like rain from heaven and the foundations of the earth will shake (***Isaiah 24:18-21***).

Jesus Himself pointed to this day. He said, "And you will see one like the Son of Man coming on the clouds of heaven" (***Mark 14:62***; ***Daniel 7:13***). Jesus will appear in the sky, and His arrival will be like a lightning strike. Only one difference – this lightning strike will be visible to everyone on earth (***Matthew 24:27***). The sun will go dark, and the stars will fall from the sky (***Matthew 24:29***).

Jesus will lead an army of angels and saints against the kings of the earth (***Revelation 19:14***). His purpose? To bring judgment on those who reject God (***2 Thessalonians 1:7-8***). When He returns, Jesus will touch down on the Mount of Olives (***Zechariah 14:4***) – just as the angels told His followers nearly two thousand years ago (***Acts 1:11***).

Then the land will split in two (***Zechariah 14:4***), and the earth will shake (***Isaiah 11:4***). Mountains will shift and move (***Revelation 6:14***). And Jesus will go out to destroy the wicked (***Isaiah 24:1***). He will physically battle the nations gathered at Armageddon (***Zechariah 14:3***).

When He encounters His enemies, a single breath from His mouth will destroy them (***Isaiah 11:4***). This isn't surprising. Jesus revealed this same power in the Garden of Gethsemane. When the Temple soldiers came to arrest Him, Jesus spoke and His words knocked them down (***John 18:6***). The same thing will happen at the Second Coming, only on a much larger scale. The Bible says His voice will cause the heavens and the earth to shake (***Joel 3:16***). His words alone will destroy the wicked (***2 Thessalonians 2:8, Revelation 19:21***).

He'll unleash the wrath of God (***Revelation 19:15***) and slaughter His enemies all over the earth (***Psalm 110:5-7***). He'll destroy the nations in His anger (***Isaiah 63:6***), and their blood will stain His clothes (***Isaiah 63:3***). He'll crush so many enemies of God their blood will form a river more than 180 miles long. This river of blood will be so deep it will reach a horse's bridle (***Revelation 14:20***). The Bible is clear. Jesus wins the Battle of Armageddon. And He wins in a blowout.

So What?

You might say, *"Okay, Britt. Maybe. Maybe not. So what? How does this concern me? I live in the here and now, not some future apocalypse. What does this have to do with my day-to-day life?"* The reason you should care is because Armageddon is not a far-off event hundreds of years in the future. It's earmarked for a specific point in human history – ***our generation.***

CHAPTER 13

When Will All These Things Happen?

One day, the Pharisees and Sadducees demanded Jesus give them a sign to prove who He was. Jesus said, "You know how to interpret the weather signs you see in the sky, but you don't know how to interpret the signs of the times. The only sign I will give you is the sign of the prophet Jonah" (*Matthew 16:1-4*).

The religious leaders of those days failed to recognize their Messiah. They failed to see Jesus for who He was. Does Jesus expect any less of us? No. He expects us to know the signs of His Second Coming. And He told us what to look for.

When the disciples asked Jesus to describe the signs of His coming and the end of the age (*Matthew 24:3*), Jesus gave them a number of signs to look for. Then He told them, "*When you see all these things*, you can know my return is near. I'm right at the door" (*Matthew 24:33*). And "*When all these things begin to happen*, look up for your salvation is near!" (*Luke 21:28*).

In other words, the top sign of His return is all the signs appearing together. Both Jesus and the prophets told us to look for those signs, and just one is reason enough to take notice. But the arrival of one sign after another? That should really get your attention. Why? Because this convergence of signs is the #1 prophetic sign – the #1 reason to believe Jesus is right at the door.

Chapter 13

THE CONVERGENCE OF SIGNS

In chapter one, we covered many of the signs Jesus and prophets said to look for. Keep in mind, generation after generation of Christians lived and died without witnessing **one** of the following signs. Yet our generation is witness to **all of them**. Those signs include:

Israel Back in the Land (*Jeremiah 16:14-15*), (*Jeremiah 23:7-8*), (*Ezekiel 39:28*), (*Isaiah 11:12*), (*Psalm 107:3*), (*Ezekiel 20:34, 41-42*), (*Isaiah 11:11-12*) – God promised to bring the Jewish people back into the land of Israel following a long, worldwide exile. The modern day nation of Israel fulfills this prophecy. God also promised to make Israel a nation again in a single day (*Isaiah 66:7-9*). This happened on May 14, 1948.

The Jews Back in Jerusalem (**Luke 21:24-28**) – Jesus said Israel's enemies would destroy the Temple and non-Jews would rule Jerusalem until "the times of the Gentiles are over." Jesus said He would come back soon after the Jews once again rule Jerusalem. For 1,897 years, people other than the Jews ruled the city. In June 1967, Israel took control of Jerusalem once again.

The Gospel Preached Throughout the World (*Matthew 24:14*), (*Revelation 14:6*) – Jesus said His message would be preached throughout the world. All the nations would hear it, and then He would return. More than any other, we take this sign for granted. Think about it. A Jewish carpenter in a tiny town in ancient Israel said His message would spread throughout the world. Unlikely to say the least. And for the first 1,500 years of Christianity, the Good News of Jesus rarely spread beyond the Mediterranean and Western Europe. But today? Today, the Gospel of Jesus is nearly everywhere. Through satellite and cable TV, the Internet, print and digital books, movies, tent revivals, and dozens of other ways, the message of Jesus reaches the most remote corners of the earth. Today, we're on the brink of seeing the Gospel preached to the whole world.

An Increase in Travel and Knowledge (*Daniel 12:4*) – Up until about 200 years ago, man had never traveled faster than a horse can gallop. And most people never traveled more than 50 miles from home. Today, we travel from one side of the earth to the other in a single day. Travel has definitely increased. And knowledge? Just look around. We've seen an explosion of knowledge in every field of endeavor.

Arrival of the Exponential Curve (*Matthew 24:3-8*) – When the disciples asked Jesus to describe the signs of His coming, he mentioned a variety of signs – spiritual, natural, societal, and political. He said these signs would appear in a distinct pattern – like "birth pains" (*Matthew 24:3-8*). Birth pains increase in both frequency and intensity in the moments leading up to birth. In other words, Jesus said the pattern of the exponential curve would mark the times. Today, we see exponential growth all around us. Population, life expectancy, technology, and other trends all follow the exponential curve.

Israel Surrounded by Enemies (*Psalm 83:4*), (*Psalm 83:12*), (*Ezekiel 11:14-17*), (*Ezekiel 35:10*) – For 1,878 years, enemies did *not* surround Israel. Why? Because the nation of Israel didn't exist. Today, Israel not only exists, but enemies surround her. These enemies say exactly what the prophets said they would. They say, "Let's wipe out the nation of Israel" (*Psalm 83:4*), "Israel and Judah are ours" (*Ezekiel 35:10*), and "the Golan Heights belong to us" (*Ezekiel 36:2*).

Israel's Exceedingly Great Army (*Ezekiel 37:10*), (*Zechariah 12:6*), (*Zechariah 12:8*) – For the first 1,900+ years of Christianity, Israel lacked an exceedingly great army. The Romans destroyed Jerusalem in A.D. 70, and Israel spent centuries in desolation. Since 1948, Israel has fought at least four conventional wars – 1948, 1956, 1967, and 1973. In each instance, enemies surrounded and outnumbered them on all sides. Yet, in each case, Israel won an overwhelming victory. Today, in spite of only being the 98th most populous nation in the world, Israel is believed to have the 15th most powerful military.

The Rise of the Gog of Magog Alliance (*Ezekiel 38:8*), (*Ezekiel 39:27*) – At no time in history have the nations of the Gog of Magog alliance worked together. Today, we see these very nations – Russia, Iran, Turkey, and others – cooperating and coordinating on military, economic, and diplomatic endeavors.

Chapter 13

The Rise of a United Europe – (*Daniel 2*), (*Daniel 7*), (*Revelation 17*) – Since the breakup of the ancient Roman Empire, many ambitious rulers have tried to reunite Western Europe. They all failed. But today, the European Union is an unstable alliance of weak and strong nations – the very characteristics Daniel claimed the final world empire would have.

The Rise of Global Government (*Revelation 13:7-17*), (*Daniel 7:23*) – Both Daniel and John said a global empire will rule the world in the end times. While this global empire hasn't appeared yet, world leaders constantly talk about global government. And with the aid of modern technology, ours is the first generation capable of realistically imagining a global empire.

Denial of the Signs (*2 Peter 3:3-4*) – Peter said people in the last days will say things like, "*I thought Jesus was coming back? What happened to His promise? Yet, since the beginning of the world, everything has remained the same!*" (*2 Peter 3:3-4*). This is exactly what we hear today, even among Christians. It's stated as fact, even though the world is remarkably different today than it was just a hundred years ago!

"But Britt," you might say. *"You keep pointing to these same signs. You're saying the same thing over and over."* That's right. I do. And you know why? Because the truth doesn't change. These signs were present yesterday, and these same signs will be present right up until the rapture. But keep this in mind – for 1,800+ years of Christianity, **none** of them were present. Today, **all** of them are.

I repeat myself because this is a message you need to hear. It's the message every Christian should brand across his heart. Advertisers say you need to hear a message at least seven times before it sinks in. I don't think it's sunk in. Too many people are asleep when it comes to recognizing the signs of His return. Jesus warned us about falling asleep (*Mark 13:26*). He told us to be awake and alert (*Matthew 25:13*).

That begs the question. Awake and alert to what? The answer is simple. **The convergence of the signs**. Because of the converging signs, we can know His return is very near. We can also know the fulfillment of all end times prophecy is also near.

TECHNOLOGY'S ROLE

With all the signs pointing to the soon return of Jesus, it's reasonable to expect some sort of spark will give rise to the Antichrist and his global empire. It's also reasonable to believe advanced technology is that spark.

The prophecies of the Bible do NOT require advanced technology for fulfillment. But we're approaching a time in the near future when new technologies will fulfill many end times bible prophecies.

Is it simply a coincidence we're seeing these technologies appear in tandem with the signs Jesus and the prophets said to look for? I don't think so. Jesus didn't say technology itself was a sign of His return. But He did say to look for the exponential curve (**Matthew 24:3-8**). And the development of technology follows an exponential curve.

Again, is it mere coincidence the signs Jesus and the prophets said to look for have converged at this exact moment in history? A moment when humanity is on the verge of unprecedented technological breakthroughs? I don't think so.

In our expected lifetime, we'll see the emergence of post-MAD weapons. Molecular manufacturing, quantum computers, and artificial intelligence could very well lead to an oppressive global empire – an empire just like the one described in **Revelation 13:7-8** and **Daniel 7:23**. These technologies could create humans so powerful they physically attack God Almighty as described in **Psalm 2:2**, **Daniel 8:25**, **Revelation 16:14**, and **Revelation 19:19**. These same breakthroughs could lead to extreme poverty (**Revelation 6:6**), opulent wealth (**Revelation 18:11-14**), and the healing of all disease (**Isaiah 35:5-6**). Is this all just a coincidence?

Again, I don't think so. And you know what else? Many predict the singularity and transhumanism will arrive in our expected lifetime. Coincidence? Again, maybe.

But maybe not.

ADVANCED TECHNOLOGY WILL LEAD TO GLOBAL GOVERNMENT

In chapter seven, we discussed post-MAD technologies and why advanced technology will lead to global government. While it's *possible* we could have global freedom and liberty in a post-MAD world, I rather doubt it. For reasons discussed earlier, I would say the odds are as close to zero as they can be.

Remember, history tells us the default form of human government is authoritarianism. Kings, queens, and dictators are the rule. Freedom, liberty, and human rights are the exception.

If it's true advanced technology will lead to global government, then the Antichrist can't appear on the world scene long after post-MAD technologies are developed. Why?

Since the Antichrist sets up his global government through conquest of nations (**Revelation 6:1-4**), more than one nation will have to exist when he comes on the world scene. Soon after the arrival of post-MAD technology, we'll have global government. Once that happens, it's too late for the Antichrist to appear. We'll already have global government, and no nations will exist for him to conquer. My point?

Either the Antichrist will appear *before* post-MAD technologies or he will appear *in tandem* with them. And since post-MAD technologies will appear sometime in our expected lifetime, we can expect the end times prophecies of the Bible to be fulfilled in the same time frame.

I'm No Prophet

At this point, you might be thinking, *"Come on, Britt. Transhumanists? Global government? Molecular manufacturing? Isn't this all just speculation on your part?"*

Yes and no. Some parts of this book (such as forecasts of technological trends) are speculative. They're based on educated guesses, and I'm sure as time goes by, some of them will seem foolish. But when it comes to bible prophecy, you can be sure everything will happen just as the Bible says.

I'm no prophet. I don't know exactly what the future holds. I don't know what day, month, or year any event will occur. What I do know is available to anyone who's willing to look to the Bible for answers. Aside from the Bible, I have no special knowledge of the future. But I do know this. Jesus said, "When you see all these things, you can know my return is near" (**Matthew 24:33**). Jesus told us to watch and look for the signs of His coming. That means we're expected to be *watchmen*. We're expected to point out these signs to others and warn them the end is near. It's our responsibility (**Ezekiel 33:1-6**).

You know what the Bible says, and as you observe world events and societal trends, you can see we live very close to the end. What ultimately matters is not *how* end times bible prophecy is fulfilled, but the certainty it *will* be fulfilled.

Technological trends and bible prophecy agree. Some say post-MAD technology will arrive no later than mid-century. If that's true, we'll have global government no later than mid-century. But regardless of whether or not technology plays a central role in the fulfillment of end times bible prophecy, you can be sure every end times prophecy will be fulfilled. And because of the converging signs, we can be sure they'll take place in our expected lifetime.

Remember, Jesus said the generation that sees these signs will not pass away before He returns (***Matthew 24:32-35***). Just as God promised Simeon he would not pass away before seeing the Messiah (***Luke 2:25-26***), God promises an entire generation they will not pass away before His return. You can be certain – Jesus is coming.

So if all this is coming to pass, what should you do? Fight technological advancement? Join in? Is technology our enemy? Both the Bible and basic observation give us the answer.

CHAPTER 14

Is Technology Our Enemy?

IN 1811, ENGLISH weavers faced the prospect of losing their jobs to machines. Some of these weavers destroyed several mechanical knitting machines in the village of Nottingham. Claiming to follow in the footsteps of a man named Ned Ludd, the protestors were given the name "Luddites." This was in honor of Ned Ludd, who they said was the first to destroy such a machine in protest of his working conditions. While Ned Ludd turned out to be nothing more than a myth, it didn't matter. The protesters proudly took on their new name.

In the years since, the term "Luddite" has become associated with a fear of new technology. It's come to mean you oppose progress. It's a term of derision.

But were the Luddites right? Were mechanical weaving looms evil? No. Mechanical looms aren't alive. They're objects. They aren't evil. And you know what? Other technologies aren't evil either. Computers aren't evil. Virtual reality isn't evil. And quantum computers, artificial intelligence, and molecular manufacturing aren't evil.

THE TRUE SOURCE OF EVIL

So why does technology sometimes *appear* to be evil? The answer is simple. It's because of the end user. Technology isn't evil. **We** *are*.

I'm no Luddite, and you shouldn't be either. We should embrace technology. Technology is a tool. It's not good, and it's not evil. But human beings? That's a different story. We *are* evil.

Each and every one of us is a sinner (***Romans 3:23***). And our sin is the

Chapter 14

root cause of evil. The problem isn't technology. It's our own wickedness. The darkness of the human heart is the world's #1 problem.

Since the Garden of Eden, every human being has been born with a sinful nature (***Psalm 51:5***). This means we're filled with evil desires, greed, jealousy, envy, pride, and a whole host of unsavory traits (***Mark 7:21-22***). And the Bible says the source of all wars and fighting is the army of evil desires at war within us (***James 4:1***). Let's face it. We're sinners. And no technology can cure us. All technology does is provide leverage. It gives us greater power. If we use that power for evil, it's not technology's fault. It's our fault.

THE HISTORY OF ADVANCED TECHNOLOGY

Don't believe me? Recent history alone should convince you.

In the 20th Century, we used advanced technology for tremendous benefit. We raised the standard of living for almost everyone in the world. We wiped out entire classes of disease. Productivity skyrocketed. The average lifespan increased. We landed men on the moon. We built telescopes to look at faraway galaxies. We made microprocessors and lifesaving drugs. We even harnessed the power of the atom. It was a great time to be alive.

But it was also a terrible time to be alive. Technology was used for evil too. Like no other time period, the 20th Century showed our capacity for mass murder and destruction. Hitler, Stalin, Mao, and others used technology to systematically murder millions. We made ever more powerful chemical, biological, and nuclear weapons. And our advances brought ever more oppressive police states in many nations.

Why is this?

In the 20th Century, advanced technology amplified our destructive nature. It magnified human evil. Will it be any different for the next generation of technology? It won't. Again, it has nothing to do with technology itself. Without a doubt, new technologies will bring great good in the years ahead. But they'll also reveal the worst of human nature. Despite all our advances, we haven't conquered human evil. We still live in a world filled with war, suffering, and death.

Our sin, combined with advanced technology, makes us more vulnerable to attacks from our real enemy – Satan and his demons. Why? Because the Bible says we are not fighting against enemies in this world. We're fighting against evil rulers and mighty powers from the unseen world (***Ephesians 6:12***).

What Will The Future Look Like?

So what will our future look like? No one knows for sure. But we can be certain of this... We'll use technology for good, and we'll use technology for evil. And as humanity pushes forward, we'll **merge** with technology. Again, in some instances this will be for the better. And in some instances, it will be for the worse.

Already, we've erased the lines between the virtual world and the real world. Soon, neuro-headset video games will bring a virtual reality so close to real life some people will never leave it. Such a world, unrestrained by social norms and offering a playground of immorality, will be fertile ground for the demons of this world. What will be the result of a virtual world where all is acceptable, because everything is "just a game"?

What will people "try out" if they don't have to worry about criminal charges? Murder... rape... torture... incest... mass murder... sexual immorality of every kind... and physical indulgence of every kind, most of it well beyond our imagination... In a virtual world, you can live out any fantasy, no matter how bizarre. And the worst part? Society will excuse it, telling us it doesn't harm anyone!

In fact, they'll say such things will **benefit** society because everyone can get their fill of violence and debauchery in the virtual world. And in the virtual world, these activities won't harm anyone.

But is this really true? What kind of a human animal will such a society produce? I'll tell you what kind of human it will produce. The kind of human who will challenge God's authority. The kind of human who will dare to take on the King of kings.

The Rich Man

Two thousand years ago, a rich man came to Jesus and asked, "What must I do to inherit eternal life?" "You know the commandments," Jesus said. "Don't commit adultery. Don't murder. Don't steal. Don't lie. And honor your father and mother."

"I've obeyed all these commandments since I was young," the rich man said. So Jesus told him, "There's one thing you still haven't done. Sell everything you own. Give the money to the poor. Then come and follow me." At this, the rich man's face fell. He walked away very sad because he had many possessions (***Mark 10:17-22***).

The rich man came face-to-face with Jesus and what did he do? He walked away. The riches of this world meant more to him. He made a choice with eternal consequences. He chose the things of this world when he could have chosen Jesus.

In our day and time, it's easy to criticize the rich man. How could he do such a thing? But we should be slow to judge. After all, we face the same choice. We can either follow Jesus or follow our own way. Unfortunately, many people reading this book will chose their own way. They'll walk away from Jesus and choose the things of this world.

Armageddon Approaches

As Armageddon approaches, more and more people will chose the path of the rich man. They'll struggle with temptations unknown to past generations. Think about it. The rich man walked away from Jesus for a ***first century*** life of luxury. We would consider his life poverty today. How much more do you have?

If you're reading this, the odds are good you live a life of luxury more extravagant than 99% of the people who have ever lived. You don't have to carry a bucket to draw water. A deluge of hot or cold water appears at your command. You can control the temperature in your house. And with relative ease, you can keep your home free of bugs and rats.

You can get any food you want from anywhere in the world. Foods rich with a variety of spices and flavors. You can go anywhere in the world you want, usually in the same day. Simply speak, and you can order almost any product and have it shipped to your front door within hours, sometimes even minutes.

Music of any type and from any time period of your choosing is instantly available whenever you want it. Endless entertainment options fight for your attention. And diseases and injuries that once meant certain death? Cured and healed because of modern medicine. I could go on and on and on…

The kings and queens of the past could only dream of these things. They didn't have a fraction of the luxuries ***you*** have today. The rich man who walked away from Jesus was poverty stricken compared to you. Yet Jesus said,

"How hard it is for the rich to enter the Kingdom of God. It's easier for a camel to go through the eye of a needle than for a rich person to enter the Kingdom of God!" (***Mark 10:23-25***).

If that's true, how much harder is it for our generation? Earthly wealth is greater than it's ever been. Now, think about this. If we live in such luxury now, how lavish will the end times world be? The Bible says the world in the end times is a place of immense wealth (***Revelation 18***).

How many people in the end times will follow in the footsteps of the rich man? Take all the wealth and opulence we have today and multiply it several times over. Imagine a world of greater abundance than you ever thought possible. A world of instantaneous travel through virtual reality.

A place where everyone is rich. No one has to work. A place where you can live out any fantasy you can imagine. A place where you'll have power beyond the wildest dreams of every king or queen. A time and place where the world will be laid at your feet. What would you do with such power?

Two thousand years ago, Satan offered such a world to Jesus. He said, "I'll give you all the kingdoms of the world. All you have to do is worship me" (***Matthew 4:9***). Jesus rebuked Satan. How many others will fall down on their knees? The Bible says the world will worship the Antichrist (***Revelation 13:4***). Many will reject God in favor of pleasure, power, and fame.

This turning away from God is what Armageddon is all about. Hollywood has distorted the truth. Armageddon isn't about asteroids or comets. It's not about nuclear war. It's about one thing and one thing only – human rebellion.

The world is racing toward Armageddon at breakneck speed. Ultimately, Armageddon is a battle between two groups:

1) Satan and his followers, and
2) Jesus and His followers

And regardless of whether you live to see Armageddon or the rise of the Antichrist, you have a choice to make. It's the same choice the rich man faced. It's the same choice every human being has faced since the dawn of creation – God's way or your way.

What will you do? Will you follow your own way? Or God's way? Jesus said if you want to save your life, you must be willing to give it up (***Matthew 16:25***).

Chapter 14

He said you're either for Him or against Him (***Luke 11:23***). He also said you can't serve both God and money (***Matthew 6:24***). This is true in every aspect of life. You can't serve both God and selfish ambition. You can't serve both God and your desires for the things of this world. Does this mean everything in the world is evil? No. But you must put God first. You must be willing to lose everything in this world. God needs to be your number one priority.

Unfortunately, I've got bad news for you. You can't do this on your own. You're in rebellion against God. Why? Because it's in your nature. In fact, it's your default setting.

THE BAD NEWS

You often hear people talk about the "good news of Jesus Christ." But "good news" implies something, doesn't it? You can't have good news unless the possibility of bad news exists, right? And the Good News has less impact unless you first understand the bad news. So what is the Bad News? The bad news is this…

You and I are born sinners. What does this mean? It means we've broken God's law. Have you ever stolen anything? Have you ever lied? Have you ever lusted in your heart? If so, you've broken God's law. You're a sinner. And let me tell you, it gets worse. God says if you break even one commandment – just one – you're guilty of breaking them all (***James 2:10***).

According to the Bible, physical and spiritual death is the penalty for sin (***Romans 6:23***). Sin separates us from a Holy God (***Isaiah 59:2***). And no good deed or series of good deeds can cover our sin.

So we have a problem here. If you die in your sins (***John 8:24***), you'll be separated from God for eternity (***2 Thessalonians 1:9***). And that means you're going to hell.

Hell is a terrible place. The Bible describes it as "a lake of fire" (***Revelation 20:15***) and a place where "blazing coals and burning sulfur rain down on the wicked" (***Psalm 11:6***). It's a place of sorrows (***Psalm 18:5***). Jesus calls it a place of torment (***Luke 16:23***), outer darkness (***Matthew 8:12***), and weeping and gnashing of teeth (***Matthew 13:42***). It's a place of no relief (***Revelation 14:11***) and eternal punishment (***Matthew 25:46***).

Hell is a terrible, terrible place. And despite what most people think, heaven is not your default destination when you die. Hell is. In rejecting God, the world is marching straight to hell. Our rebellion has placed us in direct opposition to God. Our sin condemns us to eternity in hell.

Sin is a disease. And no level of human progress will ever overcome it. Its cure isn't found among doctors, scientists, or politicians. It's not found in New Age principles or a research lab. And it's definitely not found within us.

When Adam and Eve ate the forbidden fruit, they sinned (***1 John 3:4***). They broke God's law. Their actions in the Garden of Eden infected them with sin. They passed that sin to their children, and the human race has been born into sin ever since.

I'm a sinner. You're a sinner. We're all sinners. We're born into sin. Generation after generation after generation. And on our own, there's nothing we can do about it. We can't stop sinning. Will power doesn't work. Self-discipline doesn't work. And psychology and medicine don't work.

That's bad news.

Does it mean all hope is lost?

No way. Because God has Good News.

THE GOOD NEWS

This is the Good News... Despite the fact we are sinners, God died *for* us (***Romans 5:8***). He paid the penalty for our sin so we don't have to face hell. How did He do this?

God sent His one and only Son, Jesus Christ, to be our Savior (***John 3:16-17***). He willingly went to the cross. He allowed Himself to be nailed to it. And He freely spilled His blood for you and me. The blood of Jesus wipes away our sin in the eyes of God (***1 John 1:7***). The Bible says without the shedding of blood, there is no forgiveness (***Hebrews 9:22***).

I'm a sinner. Jesus died for me. You're a sinner, and Jesus died for you. Because of Jesus, we're forgiven. We're forgiven because of God's grace. It's a free gift. It's not something you can earn through good deeds. Remember, heaven is not a place for *good* people. Heaven is a place for *forgiven* people. The Bible says God's grace saves you when you believe in His one and only Son. You're not saved as a result of good works. Otherwise you could boast (***Ephesians 2:8-9***).

That's the Good News. Not only can you avoid the horror of hell. You

Chapter 14

can enjoy all the pleasures of heaven. You can become an adopted son or daughter of Almighty God (***Ephesians 1:5***). What great news!

But there's a catch. While God's grace is freely given, you can still reject it. Only those who accept His free gift receive forgiveness. Those who reject Him die in their sins (***John 8:24***).

You can look God in the eye and tell Him you don't want or need His forgiveness. He's given everything to ransom you. He died a terrible death to save you. But He also gave you free will. He'll let you step right over His dead body and march straight into hell.

Unfortunately, untold numbers of people will do just that. Because of their pride, they'll reject God's offer. They'll refuse forgiveness of their sins, and they'll condemn themselves to eternity in hell.

Jesus said the road to hell is wide and broad and many choose it. But the gate to life is narrow and difficult and few ever find it (***Matthew 7:13-14***). Jesus is the gate (***John 10:9***). No one gets to heaven except through Him (***John 14:6***).

There is no other way to receive forgiveness for your sins (***Acts 4:12***). Only the blood of Jesus, who had no sin, can save you. Only His sacrificial death on the cross can open the door to heaven. No one else can offer a way. No one else can forgive you of sin. Buddha can't. Allah can't. Vishnu can't.

THE MOST IMPORTANT DECISION OF YOUR LIFE

That's why the most important decision of your life is whether or not to follow Jesus. It's a decision with eternal consequences.

Don't let your pride keep you from heaven. Don't trade temporary pleasure for eternity. Jesus said, "What good does it do a man to gain the whole world if he loses his soul?" (***Matthew 16:26***).

All the pleasures and material objects of this world are fleeting and meaningless. Only your relationship with God matters. The Bible says those who reject Jesus are condemned (***John 3:18***).

Are you condemned? Is your faith in Jesus or the things of this world? If you say it's in Jesus, ask yourself this... Do you know Him? Do you really know Him? Are you absolutely sure if you died right now you'd go to heaven? Take a moment and make sure you know the answer. There's nothing more important.

You may be a devoted church attendee. You may even be a pastor or a church elder. It doesn't matter. You can do all those things and still not know Jesus. Are you sure you know Him?

If you're unsure, take advantage of this moment. The Bible says now is the time. Now is the day of salvation (***2 Corinthians 6:2***). You get one life. That's it. The Bible says each person dies ***once*** and then comes judgment (***Hebrews 9:27***). Are you ready for judgment?

If you don't already know the answer, you need to decide ***today***. You have no guarantee of tomorrow. This is your moment. Long before the world began, God knew you would be right here right now reading this book. He's using it to reach you. He's calling you home. Like the father welcomed the prodigal son (***Luke 15:11-32***), he welcomes you. It doesn't matter what you've done or how many commandments you've broken. He loves you. So make your decision now.

You may think you can put off making a decision about Jesus. But if that's what you think, eventually death will make your choice for you. Remember, you don't know how much longer you have. Death could come today. And unless the rapture takes you, it will come. Everyone dies. The Bible says there's a time to be born and a time to die (***Ecclesiastes 3:2***). Adam and Eve died. Alexander the Great died. Julius Caesar died. Aristotle, Shakespeare, Mozart, Einstein, and Gandhi all died. And you'll die too.

Are you ready? Jesus said, "I am the way and the truth and the life. No one comes to the Father except through me" (***John 14:6***). Jesus was either a liar, insane, or He was what He said. Which one do you think He was?

If I were you, I would make up my mind right now. Because Jesus said if you're not for Him, you're against Him (***Luke 11:23***). That means even if Armageddon is years away, you're already in direct conflict with God. That's right. If you're not for Jesus, you're ***already*** in direct conflict with God. There's no in between. You can't have it both ways.

God has given you free will to choose your own eternal destiny. Will your blood stain His garments (***Isaiah 63:3***), or will His blood cleanse you of sin and bring you eternal life (***1 John 1:7***)? The choice is yours alone, but make no mistake - Jesus is coming! And when He comes, there will be nowhere to hide (***Revelation 6:15-16***).

Solomon said the purpose of life is to fear God and obey His commands, then the judgment comes (***Ecclesiastes 12:13-14***). Regardless of whether you

Chapter 14

live to see Armageddon or not, judgment will come. And regardless of whether you die today or half a century from now, judgment will come. The Book of Revelation says a day is coming when the earth and sky will flee His presence (**Revelation 20:11**). The people of the earth will have nowhere to hide.

On that day, anyone whose name is not found in the Book of Life will be thrown into the lake of fire (**Revelation 20:11-15**). But those who trust in Jesus will awake to everlasting life (**Matthew 25:46**). Do you want to be thrown into a lake of fire? Me neither. But that's what the Bible says is coming if you reject Jesus. Doesn't "awakening to everlasting life" sound much better? It does.

The world is racing toward Armageddon. But you don't have to race with it. When Jesus steps on the battlefield, there will be two armies – those who are for Him and those who are against Him. Which group will you be in?

ABOUT THE AUTHOR

Britt Gillette is a devoted follower of Jesus Christ, husband to Jen, and father to Samantha and Tommy. He and his family live in Virginia.

Britt is also the author of:

Coming To Jesus:
One Man's Search for Truth and Life Purpose

Signs Of The Second Coming:
11 Reasons Jesus Will Return in Our Lifetime

Spread the Word
Word-of-mouth is crucial for any book to succeed and reviews have enormous influence. If you've enjoyed this book, I would be very grateful if you could spend just five minutes posting a review on Amazon, Kobo, iBooks, Barnes & Noble, GoodReads, or your favorite book review site. Even if it's only a sentence or two, it would make a world of difference and would be very much appreciated.

Also, please share this book with others. You can make a difference in someone's life today by sharing the Good News of Jesus Christ.

Come Visit Us on the Web
Britt writes a number of articles about Jesus Christ and bible prophecy on his website, www.end-times-bible-prophecy.com. Please drop by and visit! You can also connect with him on Facebook at www.facebook.com/brittgilletteauthor.

CPSIA information can be obtained
at www.ICGtesting.com
Printed in the USA
LVHW100533220420
654274LV00009B/657

9 781981 968701